Michael Ferrebee Sadler

The sacrament of responsibility

Testimony of Scripture to the teaching of the church on holy baptism

CONTENTS.

CONTENTS.

The Sacrament of Responsibility.

A DIALOGUE.

C. I was glad to see you at Church yesterday, and still more so, to observe that you seemed very attentive to the service.

D. I was pleased with the solemn and reverential manner in which the worship of God was conducted. There were some expressions in the service, however, which appeared to me to be unscriptural; and I have now come for the purpose of having some friendly discourse with you upon them.

C. Being myself thoroughly persuaded of the agreement of every part of our Prayer-Book with the word of God, I shall be most thankful if God should enable me to remove any misconception from your mind. What expressions struck you as being unscriptural?

D. Some parts of the service your Minister used when he was baptizing that infant after the chapter read from the New Testament. He read with a loud voice after he had baptized it in the name of the Trinity— "Seeing now, dearly beloved brethren, that this child "is regenerate, and grafted into the body of Christ's "Church." How could he tell that it was regenerate? what right had he to say any such thing? Surely he must have had many misgivings in using such words, but as they were appointed, I suppose he had no choice about the matter.

C. I can well understand your expressing yourself so strongly on this subject, for I once thought pretty nearly the same.

D. I should like to know what altered your opinion.

C. My opinion was changed by reading the Scriptures.

D. Do you mean to say that by reading the Scriptures *only,* you came to believe that all children are *regenerate* when baptized ?

C. Yes; I do mean to say that my study of God's word has led me to believe, that the child you saw baptized yesterday was there and then "born of water and the spirit," that is, washed from the guilt of his birth sin, incorporated into Christ the second Adam, clothed with Him, counted by Almighty God as buried and raised again in His Son, and made a partaker of His Spirit — in the words of our Baptismal service, "REGENERATE AND GRAFTED INTO THE BODY OF CHRIST'S CHURCH;" or, in the words of our Catechism, "MADE A MEMBER OF CHRIST, THE CHILD OF GOD, AND AN INHERITOR OF THE KINGDOM OF HEAVEN."

D. You think then, that every child, at its baptism, has that vital change of heart given to it, that will *necessarily* make it live to Christ here, and enjoy His glory in the world to come.

C. I think no such thing.

D. But did you not say that you believed that each child was *regenerated and grafted into the body of Christ's Church* when baptised ? Surely that implies that the child will grow up a true Christian.

C. According to my view, it does not necessarily imply this. Can there be no such thing as a barren branch in a fruitful vine ? or a barren and worthless graft on a good stock ?

D. Certainly; but you would not apply this to spiritual grafting into Jesus Christ ?

C. I must so apply it, for Jesus Christ has taught me to do so in St John's Gospel, *chap.* xv. where I read — "I am the true vine, and my Father is the "husbandman. Every branch IN ME that beareth not "fruit He taketh away," evidently implying that a branch may be for a time in Him, and yet barren and unprofitable. I believe that that child was then grafted into Christ, but whether he afterwards bear fruit to God's glory depends on his "*abiding in Him.*" If he grows up ungodly, it is no reason for denying that he was once grafted into Christ, just as the unfruitfulness of a particular branch of a vine is no reason for denying that it is joined to the stem, and receives its nourishment from it. If a graft produced no fruit, you could not on that account say that it never had been grafted into the stock, but only that it had been grafted to no purpose.

D. I perceive, by what you say, that we attach different meanings to the word "Regeneration."

C. It certainly appears that we do, and this will be found the source of much misunderstanding on this subject. The change which you call *Regeneration* or *New Birth*, I call, *Conversion*. The Church is, and always has been, most careful in not confounding Regeneration with any after-change, however necessary that change may be, and I think we shall find that she has good Scripture reasons for so doing.

D. What explanation then do you give of this most important word 'Regeneration'?

C. Regeneration, or New Birth, is the Covenant-blessing, or Inward and spiritual grace that God has attached to the Sacrament of Baptism. Conversion, is the act of a penitent soul turning from sin and Satan to God and holiness, and may take place before, in, or after Baptism: In the case of an adult, Conversion must precede Baptism, or the Sacrament is profaned: In the case of a person who has been baptized in Infancy, and who has neglected or despised his Baptismal engagements, and grieved the Spirit then given to him, Conversion must take place after Baptism, or the man never can enjoy the happiness of heaven.

I believe, that the child, which you saw baptized yesterday, was washed from the guilt of his original sin, grafted into Christ's mystical body, and made a partaker of His Spirit. This was his Regeneration or New Birth: but still, I believe that, that child, if he grow up from his earliest years ever so full of God's faith and fear, will still have need continually to pray God in some such words as those of our Collect for Christmas Day: "that he being regenerate, and made God's child by adoption and grace, may daily be renewed by God's Holy Spirit." If, as is the case with such a lamentably large proportion of those baptized in Infancy, he grow up unholy, and impenitent, he will have to be converted, *i. e.* he will have to turn from sin and Satan to God and holiness, or he will assuredly never enjoy that inheritance of which he was, in and by Baptism, made an heir.

A 2

D. But still I cannot understand what Scripture grounds you have for believing that all children are, at their baptisms, grafted into Christ's body, the Church, and made partakers of His Spirit,—that they are made partakers of those glorious privileges you just now recounted.

C. As I said before, I shall be most thankful if God enable me to set the truth convincingly before you, and as He alone can enable us to understand His word, let us both kneel down, and offer up a prayer for the guidance of His Spirit.

D. With all my heart.

C. " God who didst teach the hearts of thy faithful " people by the sending to them the light of thy Holy " Spirit; grant us by the same Spirit to have a right " judgment in all things, and evermore to rejoice in " his holy comfort; through the merits of Christ Jesus " our Saviour, who liveth and reigneth with thee, in " the unity of the same Spirit, one God, world without " end. Amen."

D. What an appropriate prayer!

C. I took it from the Prayer-book. It is the collect we use on Whitsunday. But to proceed. As I told you before, I once thought much the same as you do on this subject, and the circumstances by which I was led, by God's blessing, to see my error, were the following.— When our present pastor came into the parish, one of the first acts of his ministry was to baptize my youngest infant. The week after, he called upon me, and requested me to become a teacher in his Sunday School. I told him I would gladly do so, but understood that he required all the children to learn the Church Catechism, which I said, I could not conscientiously teach them. He enquired my reason with some surprise, and I answered, that as I could not teach my own children to say, that *in their baptism* they were made members of Christ and children of God, I could not teach others to do so. Upon this, my wife brought all our children into the room, which, for a time, interrupted the conversation; he talked to them on religious subjects suited to their tender years, and asked those who were able, to say the Lord's Prayer, which they did. After they had left the room, he reverted to the subject, and enquired, how I could have joined in the thanksgiving of the Baptismal service of my own child, in which were rendered hearty thanks to God that He had made the infant His own child by adoption? I told him I had done so on the charitable supposition that it was so made; but that I should like the service much better if such strong expressions were not used in it. 'How strangely inconsistent you are' he replied. You refused to thank God at your child's baptism, that it was made His child by adoption, you refuse to teach it the catechism, because it has to say therein "my Baptism wherein I was made a member of "Christ, the child of God;" and yet you teach it daily to say in prayer to God, "Our Father." 'Yes,' I rejoined, 'but is it not somewhere written in Scripture that we are God's children by faith?' 'It is,' he replied, 'but do you know the context of the passage to which you refer?' I was obliged to confess that I did not. 'Well,' he said, 'here is a New Testament; look in *Galatians* iii. 27., and you will read "Ye are all the children of God by faith in "Christ Jesus, *for* as many of you as have been baptised "into Christ, have put on Christ."' To this I answered 'Does not this refer to persons who received the sacrament of Baptism as adults?' 'Can we apply it to infants who have not faith?'— He replied, 'can we baptize them at all?' If their want of faith, through their tender years, hinders them from receiving baptismal grace and privilege, let us delay their baptism till we are assured of their faith;— If God has mercifully allowed us to baptize them notwithstanding their tender years and consequent want of faith;—If His Son has said, "Suffer "the little children to come unto Me," and bid us not despise them, for "of such is the kingdom of God,"— that it is not the will of His Father that *one* of these little ones should perish;—are we at liberty to suppose any of them deprived of the inward grace of the Sacrament?— that God makes it *on His part*, in the vast majority of cases, a mere ceremony, an empty sign? Had the Galatian Christians no children? If they had, did they baptize them? If they did, did the baptism of these Galatian children make the words of the Apostle applicable to them, or not? I felt I could answer nothing to all this, it was so different from anything I had ever heard before. 'How is it,' he then said, 'that you did not come to me about this? I am always anxious that my people should bring their difficulties to me, and

I would do what lay in my power to solve them.' I told him I had thought of doing so, but was deterred, from the feeling, that it was not a matter of sufficient consequence, for I did not like to ask his explanation of points connected, as I conceived, with a mere form or ceremony. 'I am afraid,' he rejoined, 'you have thought little about Baptism, if you so speak of it. Are you aware that the doctrine of Baptism is classed by the Apostle St Paul among the "first principles" of the doctrine of Jesus Christ, "the foundation of the faith?" In *Hebrews* vi. the Holy Spirit mentions six principles or foundations of the doctrine of Christ; "Repentance," "Faith," the doctrine of "Baptism," and of "Laying on of hands," "Resurrection from the dead," and "Eternal judgment." Ask your own common sense, can that doctrine be of small importance which is classed as a first principle with *repentance, faith* and *judgment to come?* And then, as regards its practical tendency, are you aware that St Paul, in three of his Epistles, makes the doctrine of Baptism. the strongest motive he can urge upon Christians to live holy lives? (*Romans* vi. *Coloss.* ii. iii. 1 *Corinthians* x. 1—12.). Are you aware that the Scriptures tell us that the Apostle St Paul himself was not cleansed from his sins till he partook of the Sacrament of Baptism, which God had ordained for that purpose? After his conversion, after his prayers, after three days and nights of agony and fasting, he was told to "arise, and be baptized, and wash away his sins," calling on the name of the Lord." Evidently implying, that even *his* sins were not done away till he came to the ordinance, appointed by the Lord, for the communication of the cleansing efficacy of His blood.'

I was obliged to confess to him that all this was entirely new to me. I felt it to be a matter on which I had thought little or nothing, and I perceived from the passages of the Word of God he had brought before me that it required my most serious attention. He then gave me a list of Scripture texts, all bearing on the subject, and urged me to examine them with prayer for the guidance of that Spirit, Who alone can lead to all truth. I will read them over to you.

D. With all my heart. I know one or two passages in which very exalted language is applied to Baptism. I once mentioned them to my religious teacher, and he told me not to think any thing of them, as he said they were metaphorical, or hypothetical, or figurative, or used some such expression respecting them.

C. If God tells us anything plainly and distinctly, we must take good heed that we do not fritter away the meaning of what He says by applying to it such terms as metaphorical, hypothetical, figurative, &c.

Here are the passages,

I. *St John's Gospel* iii. 3—5. "Except a man be born again, "he cannot see the kingdom of God. Nicodemus saith "unto him, How can a man be born when he is old? can "he enter the second time into his mother's womb, and be "born? Jesus answered, Verily, verily, I say unto thee, "except a man be born *of water, and of the Spirit,* he "cannot enter the kingdom of God."

II. *St Matthew* xxviii. 19, 20. "Go ye therefore, and teach all "nations, baptizing them in the name of the Father, and of "the Son, and of the Holy Ghost: teaching them to observe "all things whatsoever I have commanded you: and, lo, I "am with you alway, even unto the end of the world."

III. *St Mark* xvi. 16. "He that believeth, and is *baptized* shall "be saved; but he that believeth not shall be damned."

IV. *Acts* ii. 37—39. "Men and brethren, what shall we do? "Then Peter said unto them, Repent, and be *baptized* every "one of you in the name of Jesus Christ, *for the remission* "*of sins,* and ye shall receive the gift of the Holy Ghost. "For the promise is unto you, and to your children, &c."

V. *Acts* xxii. 10. and 16. "And I said, what shall I do, Lord? "And the Lord said unto me, Arise, and go into Damascus; "and there it shall be told thee of all things which are "appointed for thee to do.—And now, why tarriest thou? "arise, and *be baptized,* and *wash away thy sins,* calling on "the name of the Lord."

VI. *Romans* vi. 1, 2, 3, 4. "What shall we say then? Shall "we continue in sin, that grace may abound? God forbid. "How shall we, that are dead to sin, live any longer therein? "Know ye not, that *so many* of us as were baptized into "Jesus Christ were baptized into his death? *Therefore we* "*are buried with him by baptism into death:* that like as "Christ was raised up from the dead by the glory of the "Father, even so we also should walk in newness of life."

VII. *Colossians* ii. 12, 13. "*Buried with him in Baptism, wherein* "also *ye are risen* with him through the faith of the opera-"tion of God, who hath raised him from the dead. And "you, being dead in your sins, and the uncircumcision of "your flesh, hath he quickened together with him, having "forgiven you all trespasses. iii. 1. If ye then be *risen* with "Christ, seek those things which are above, where Christ "sitteth on the right hand of God. Set your affection on "things above, not on things on the earth. *For ye are* "*dead,* and your life is hid with Christ in God."

VIII. *Ephesians* v. 25, 26. "Husbands, love your wives, even as "Christ also loved the Church, and gave himself for it, that "he might sanctify and cleanse it with the *washing of water* "by the word."

IX.   *Titus* iii. 5. "Not by works of righteousness which we have "done, but according to his mercy he saved us, by the "*washing of Regeneration*, and renewing of the Holy Ghost."

X.   *Galatians* iii. 26, 27. "For ye are all the children of God "by faith in Christ Jesus. For *as many of you* as have "been *baptized* into Christ have put on Christ."

XI.   *Hebrews* x. 21, 22. "Having an High-priest over the house "of God; let us draw near with a true heart, in full "assurance of faith, having our hearts sprinkled from an "evil conscience, and our *bodies washed with pure water*."

XII.   1 *St Peter* iii. 21. "The like figure whereunto, even *Bap-* "*tism, doth also now save us* (not the putting away of the "filth of the flesh, but the answer of a good conscience "towards God,) by the resurrection of Jesus Christ."

XIII.   1 *Corinthians* x. 1, 2, 3, 4, 5, 6. 11. "Moreover, brethren, "I would not that ye should be ignorant, how that *all* our "Fathers were under the cloud, and *all* passed through the "sea; and were *all baptized* unto Moses in the cloud and "in the sea; and did *all* eat the same spiritual meat; and "did *all* drink the same spiritual drink; for they drank of "that spiritual rock that followed them; and that rock was "Christ, &c." "Now all these things happened unto them "for ensamples; and they are written for our admonition, "upon whom the ends of the world are come."

XIV.   1 *Corinthians* xii. 12, 13. 27. "For as the body is one, and "hath many members, and all the members of that one "body, being many, are one body; so also is Christ. *For by* "*one Spirit are we all baptized* into one body, whether we "be Jews or Gentiles, whether we be bond or free; and "have been all made to drink into one Spirit. * * * Now "*ye* are the body of Christ and members in *particular*."

Here are fourteen passages in which *salvation, or remission of sins, union with Christ, or being grafted into Christ's body*, are connected with Baptism; I might have added several more, but I was desirous to confine myself to passages containing a direct allusion to the Sacrament.

D. I allow that many of these passages seem to favour the doctrine you draw from them; respecting some, however, I am not able to see in what way you make them support your view. I grant that the greater part do connect salvation in some way or other with Baptism; still, two objections occur to my mind respecting them; one is, that a number of other passages may be brought of a contrary tendency; the other, that they refer to the Baptism of adults,—believing Christians of mature age, and not to that of infants.

C. As to your first objection.—To do away with the force of what our Lord says to Nicodemus respecting Baptism, one must be expressly told that, in spite of our Lord's own words, a man need *not* be "born of water and of the spirit" to enter into the kingdom of God. Again, with reference to *Acts* xxii. 16.; if we could find it any where asserted, that St Paul was cleansed from his sins before his Baptism—when he first repented, or prayed, for instance—then we might say that one passage was neutralized by another, but which, I ask, should we then be called upon to believe? And so with respect to *Romans* vi. 1—4., if in another passage of that epistle we found, that *not all* the Romans who had been baptized, had been "buried with Christ" in Baptism, that *not* "*so many of* "*them* as had been baptized into Jesus Christ had been baptized into His death," and consequently "buried with "Him by Baptism into death, that like as He was raised "from the dead by the glory of the Father, even so they "also should walk in newness of life," but only *a part of them*, who lived answerably to their Christian profession, had been so co-buried and co-raised with Him;— then there would be a real contradiction in the Apostle's words. But mark what would be the consequence: St Paul is arguing against the abuse of God's grace, and he uses an argument that reaches *all* to whom he addresses himself. *All* were in his view buried with Christ in Baptism, *i. e.* Baptism communicated to all a real interest in Christ's death, made them partakers of it, in order that all the baptized might "walk in newness of life." If only a part of them had been buried with Christ in their Baptism, the great motive to *all* to live holy lives, which the apostle urges from the fact of *each one's Baptism* being a burial with Christ into death, would not be applicable to *all*. The men who were inclined to abuse God's grace by continuing in sin that grace might abound would say,—'This does not apply 'to us. Baptism, in our case, was only a form. *It con-* '*veyed no grace for which we are responsible.* We may 'now live on according to the dictates of our natural 'hearts, until we receive some future Baptism of the 'Spirit to give us a saving interest in Christ.'

D. Do not think I would willingly disparage any one passage of God's Word; but I am not convinced that all these passages refer to the *outward rite* of Baptism. May not some of them allude to a baptism of the Spirit independent of the application of water?

C. Let us take the first of these passages; our Lord's words to Nicodemus; "Except a man be born of water "and of the Spirit, he cannot enter into the kingdom "of God." If our Lord here does not allude to Baptism by water, to what can He possibly allude? He cannot surely intend to mislead his Church by connecting the new birth with water, if water has nothing to do with the new birth, *i. e.* if God does not make it His instrument for conveying the grace of *Regeneration.* If the passage alludes to spiritual conversion at some period of life when the reasoning powers are fully developed, some change *of hopes, views, affections, and desires,* (which in *modern* phrase is called *regeneration,*) why does our Lord mention water at all; for, according to *your* view of these matters, water is no agent in affecting this? and mark, too, what is most important, that the mention of water occurs in the second answer of our Lord to Nicodemus, not in the first. Our Lord *first* answered Nicodemus by saying, "Except a man be born again, he cannot see the kingdom of God;" and when Nicodemus asks for an explanation, in the words "How can a man be born when "he is old?" Our Lord *then* answered, "Except a man "be born of water, and of the Spirit, he cannot enter into "the kingdom of God." He explains being *"born again,"* by the phrase *"being born of water and of the Spirit."* If the order had been inverted;—if our Lord had said in the *first* instance, "Except a man be born of water, and of the Spirit, he cannot enter into the kingdom of God," and, on Nicodemus asking for an explanation, He had said, "Except a man be born again—" omitting all mention of water,—in that case it might be said, that our Lord intended to qualify His previous assertion, so as to make the outward sign, *in all cases,* not necessary to the new birth. But the passage in the word of God is exactly the contrary, and leads us to a conclusion from which we cannot possibly escape.

D. But does it follow from our Lord's words that the birth of water and of the Spirit must take place at the same time—the time of Baptism? May not a man be born of "water" at one time, and of the "Spirit" at some subsequent period?

C. Impossible. "To be born" is in every case one distinct event taking place at a definite moment. And as our Lord explains being *"born again,"* by being *"born of water and of the Spirit,"* if He means one thing by the first expression, "being born again," He must mean but one thing by the second expression, "being born of

water and of the Spirit." And again, I may ask, if such
is His meaning: that a man may be born of water at one
time and of the Spirit at another—why should He mention
the birth of water at all? If it be so insignificant in itself,
and, *according to your principles*, so utterly unconnected
with any spiritual change, what reason can we assign
for His mentioning it in the same breath with that
spiritual change of feelings, affections, hopes, and desires,
in fact, of the whole inner man, which you denominate
regeneration?

D. But I have read in a commentary, that to be
"born of water and of the Spirit" means to be born
of the "Spirit acting like water." Do you not think
the words of our Lord may bear that meaning?

C. I think upon such a principle of interpretation
you may make the Word of God mean anything you
choose. If our Lord meant that, He would have said it.
Words were not wanting to Him Who made the tongue
itself, and gave to man his faculty of speech. Our Lord
is telling Nicodemus how he is to enter into His kingdom,
and surely in a matter of such importance, he would not
use language that required to be altered before it could
be received or understood. Such a meaning was never
heard of in the Church for 1500 years.

D. But this is only one of fourteen passages. I do
not clearly see that all the others bear you out in your
view of Baptism, indeed one or two strike me as opposed
to it rather than otherwise.

C. In the passages from *St Matthew* xxviii., and
St Mark xvi., Baptism is distinctly enjoined as necessary
to salvation; and surely the fact that our Lord commanded it just before His ascension, at His last interview
with His disciples, stamps it as of no ordinary importance. *There must be some great mystery of grace attending a Sacrament enjoined in the very few parting words
of our Lord to His disciples.*

D. But does not our Lord's omission of the mention
of Baptism, in the latter clause of the passage from
St Mark, shew that He did not mean to make it indis-
pensible? He does not say, "He that believeth not,"
and is not baptized.

C. How could He say any such thing? A man
that did not believe would either not be baptized at all,
or his Baptism, being in unbelief, would be a sacrament

of condemnation to him, rather than of salvation. Our Lord pre-supposes that they who believe in Him, will submit to be saved in His way.

To proceed from these to the two passages, *Acts* ii. 37—39; xxii. 16. In both, Baptism is enjoined for *remission of sins*, not of course independent of right dispositions to prepare men for it, but as the appointed instrument for the conveyance of the saving effects of Christ's blood to those who repent and believe. With these two we may class *Ephesians* v. 26; where Christ is said to "cleanse His Church *with the washing of water* by the word*."* Here then are three passages, all bearing out the doctrine of our Creed, "I acknowledge one Baptism for the remission of sins." To these we may add *Titus* iii. 5.—" By His mercy He saved us, by the "*washing of regeneration*, and renewing of the Holy " Ghost."*

D. That is one of the passages to your use of which I object. May not "the *washing of regeneration*" mean the inward application of the Spirit to purify the heart, independent of any outward Baptism with water?

O. Not on your principles. You hold, I suppose, the leading outlines of what is popularly called, ' The Calvinistic system?'

D. I do.

O. Well then, according to the divines of that School, *Regeneration* is not a washing, but an entire change of principles, desires, affections, and hopes, which has nothing to do with remission of sins, but must rather be kept totally distinct from it. It is considered the most dangerous of all errors to confound them, and the man who does so in the slightest degree, is held by persons of your school, to be utterly in the dark respecting the first principles of religious knowledge. The work of the Lord Jesus in *washing* from sin, *i. e. Justification*, and the work of the Spirit in *Sanctification* are not to be confounded, and against such as do so, that system directs its direst anathemas.

The teaching of the Church, on the contrary, makes such a passage as this plain and intelligible. We hold

---

* This place is interpreted as applying to Baptism by Luther, Calvin, Beza, Jewel, Hooker, Bp. Hall, Barrow, Jeremy Taylor, Beveridge, Mede, Wesley, Alford.

that Jesus Christ is now present in His Church by His Spirit, and by that Spirit he applies all the effects of His Cross and Passion to individual believers; that consequently, in Baptism, the Spirit sanctifies water to the "mystical washing away of sin," so that when the Sacrament is administered, inasmuch as what the minister does he does in the name of the Trinity, it is not he who baptizes, but Christ Himself, by His Spirit, according to His promise, "lo, I am with you alway, even unto the "end of the world." In this way we are enabled to recognize that Baptism is now, what it was at the beginning, a Sacrament for the remission of sins, and grafting into Christ's body, and the adoption of the person baptized into the family of God;—in other words, the Sacrament of Regeneration. And we find, in confirmation of this, that the Church in its earliest and purest times held the same view, and invariably interpreted this text, and that in our Lord's discourse with Nicodemus, as referring to the Baptismal washing in which the Spirit applies the blood of the Saviour for the remission of sins.

To proceed—in *Galatians* iii. 26., Baptism is a *putting on* of Christ, in which (according to Luther's exposition of the passage) the Christian puts on Christ evangelically; he clothes himself with Christ's righteousness, and this he states is done in Baptism.

D. There are yet three other passages that I should like to see more clearly how you apply to your purpose. Two of them are those in which Baptism is spoken of as a death, burial, and resurrection with our Saviour. I always thought that the expressions in *Romans* vi. 1—4. *Coloss.* ii. 12, 13, were merely figurative, or typical, that they taught baptized persons that they *ought* to die continually to sin and rise to newness of life.

C. So they do, but how do they teach this? By assuring us, that Baptism was the means by which we were, each one for himself, savingly united to Christ in His death to sin and resurrection to a new or justified life. Christ died for sin, for the sins of the whole world, and each one of us, if we would not everlastingly suffer the penalty of our own sins, in our own persons, must suffer the penalty of that sin *in Christ*, and be absolved from it in *Him*. This, the Apostle expressly asserts, is done for us in the Sacrament of Baptism. It is the appointed instrument by which we are made partakers of His death and resurrection. "Know ye not that "so many of us as were baptized into Jesus Christ, were "baptized into His death. Therefore we are *buried with* "*Him by Baptism into death*, that, like as Christ was "raised from the dead by the glory of the Father, "even so we also should walk in newness of life." "*Buried with Him in Baptism wherein* also ye are "risen with Him through the faith of the operation of "God, who hath raised Him from the dead. And "you, being dead in your sins, and the uncircumcision "of your flesh, hath he quickened together with Him, "having forgiven you all trespasses." See then the force and beauty of the Apostle's argument. He is reasoning against those who would pervert the grace of Christ to the indulgence of sin. He appeals to them on the ground of what took place at their solemn admission into the Christian covenant. They were then co-buried and co-raised with Christ. When they went under the water, and rose again, it was not a simple bath, or washing, but a SACRAMENTAL *death, burial,* and *resurrection* with the Saviour. They went, as it were, into the tomb with Christ, when they went under the water of Baptism, and rose from the tomb with Him when they came out, and were, by doing so, accounted as having died and risen again with Him, freed as completely from *past* sin, as a dead man is, who has suffered the penalty of death for sin, but, unlike him, freed from sin to live again to God, if so be that they did not go counter to their baptismal rising again; which the Apostle's argument implies that they might do. They were then *new creatures in Christ,* (by virtue of their union with Him who died once for all for sin,) just as we say, that a man who is discharged from prison, free from debt, is a new man: he can begin life anew, freed from the pressure of his old burdens. Christ had died for sin in their stead, and risen again, and they had been made partakers of His death and resurrection. He died to sin once, but He rose again and lived to God. So was it with them. They were to *reckon themselves dead indeed unto sin, but alive unto God through Jesus Christ our Lord.* If they again returned to the service of sin, they committed an act as outrageous as if a criminal, who had once been sentenced for a crime, and had escaped the sentence of the law, because an innocent person had voluntarily chosen to suffer in his stead, should, notwithstanding this, again commit the same act from the consequence of which he had been so mercifully delivered.

D. The exposition you give of this important passage is almost entirely new to me.

C. That is because your reading has been confined to expositors who consider that to be merely *figurative*, which the Apostle declares to be *real*, and who teach us, that when the Apostle asserts that we *have* died to sin in Christ, at some past time, he merely means we *ought* to die to sin in ourselves at some future time. They know full well that if they take the verses as they stand, in the words of the Holy Ghost, it would destroy their whole system. It may assist you in understanding this important passage to remember, that the key to it is in the first and second verses of the chapter. St Paul there appeals to men not to *continue · in sin* because they *are dead*, or rather (as the original has it) *have died to sin.* This death to sin may be either a *Sacramental* death in Baptism, by a Sacramental union with Christ's death; or a death of affection and desire, so that the person so dead has no stirring of an evil nature within him, as the limbs of a dead man stir not. That it does *not* mean the latter is evident from the persons against whom the Apostle is arguing, men who would continue in sin that grace might abound, and who· surely could not, *in that sense*, be called dead to sin; it must then mean the former, and with this the whole chapter harmonizes.

D. There is yet another passage, 1 *Corinthians* x. 1, 2, 3, 4, &c. What doctrine respecting Baptism do you. gather from this?

C. The same that I gather from half the others; that it is a present deliverance from the guilt of sin, and an entrance into a state of Salvation, which Salvation, however, is to be " worked out with fear and trembling," or we shall not finally enjoy that eternal Salvation, for the attainment of which we have been already *saved* at our entrance into the Church of Christ. St Paul saw with sorrow that many among the Corinthians were not walking worthy of their vocation; they trusted that, having been once washed from sin, and engrafted into Christ, they would be finally saved without strenuous

efforts on their own part. He writes to disabuse them of
so gross an error. At the end of the preceding chapter,
the ninth, he tells them that so far from feeling sure
of *his own* salvation, he kept under his body, and brought
it into subjection, lest, having preached to others, he
himself should become a cast-away. He then proceeds,
(in the tenth chapter) to stir up the Corinthian Christians
to wholesome fear respecting themselves. He does this
by bringing before them the example of the deliverance
of the children of Israel out of Egypt, the greater part
of whom, so delivered, perished, through their own
repeated sin, before they arrived at the promised land.
St Jude, in his Epistle, in a similar passage, applies
the word "saved" to the deliverance of the Israelites;
"I will therefore put you in remembrance, though ye
"once knew this, how that the Lord, *having saved*
"the people out of the land of Egypt, afterwards de-
"stroyed them that believed not." Both Apostles, then,
bring before their converts the example of a multitude of
persons, whom God *saved*, and yet they finally attained
not the end for which He saved them. He saved them
from Egyptian bondage, from Pharaoh and his host,
and brought them into the wilderness for the very
purpose of giving them the promised land, but in the
words of the Psalmist, "they thought scorn of that
"pleasant land, and gave no credence unto His word."
The Apostle would warn the Corinthians by their example, but how is he to do this? The salvation of
the Israelites was a salvation from slavery in brickkilns,
from a bondage of the outward man; the salvation of
the Corinthians was, on the contrary, of a spiritual nature,
altogether from spiritual foes, from the guilt and punishment of sin. How then can St Paul shew any likeness
between these two salvations, so as to make the one
a figure or type of the other, and thus induce his
Corinthian converts to "take heed" after the example
of the Israelites? One being, so to speak, a salvation
in the visible; the other in the invisible world. He
does so in this way. You observe how he uses the
word *all*,—"*all* our Fathers"—"*all* passed through
the Sea,—"*all* were baptized." Now between *all* the
Israelites and *all* the Corinthian Christians there was
but one point of resemblance, and that we may call a
Sacramental one. Every Israelite, without exception,

was baptized to Moses in the Red sea, every Corinthian Christian was baptized into Christ. St Paul seizes on this one resemblance for his purpose. The Baptism of the Israelites in the Red Sea was their salvation; it was the thing by which, and the moment at which they were saved from Pharaoh; and all, without exception, who partook of the Red Sea Baptism were thus saved, those who perished in the Wilderness equally partook of the salvation with those few who resisted the temptations of the Wilderness, passed Jordan, and entered into rest. The Baptism of the Corinthians must have been . *to each one of them* a corresponding salvation, a salvation answering to the different dispensation under which they lived, or St Paul could not possibly have brought the *whole body* of the Israelites as an example to the *whole body* of the Corinthian Church. If the Corinthians had not *all* been brought into a real state of salvation at their Baptism, how could any comparison be instituted between them and a body of men, *all* of whom had, at *their Baptism*, been so signally delivered from bondage and death, and translated into liberty?

Does not this shew us, that if we deprive the Sacrament of what God has joined to it, viz. its saving grace, we deprive ourselves of the power of making use of it as a motive to holiness; and that if we restrict the reception of grace to those who afterwards improve that grace, we are utterly unable to apply the Sacrament, as a motive to holiness, to those to whom the Apostle applied it, that is, to those who most needed it—to men who, so far from improving grace given, were tampering with idolatry, and defiling their bodies with gross sin? Such as these St Paul was alluding to when he wrote this part of his Epistle, for he had said a little before to these same persons, "Flee fornication," (chap. vi. 18.), and in the fourteenth verse of this chapter, "Flee from idolatry," and both on the same ground, that they had been made "the body of Christ." (chap. x. 17.). If the Baptism of such as these had been of no present efficacy, as some would assert, because they afterwards shewed themselves to be unstable, or sensual, how could the Apostle have made the use of it he did? His argument for *present* holiness, because of *past* deliverance, AND THE RESPONSIBILITY THEREBY INCURRED, would fall to the ground, and be utterly inapplicable

to the case of the very individuals for whose especial
warning he was writing at the time.

D. I thank you sincerely for your pains in explaining these important passages; but do they not refer
to the Baptism of persons who at the time when they
were baptized, were adults, and understood the nature
of the rite? Can we apply the doctrine contained in
them, with equal certainty, to those baptized in Infancy?

C. Before we enter upon this part of the subject,
allow me to ask,—Do you in your heart believe that
the blessings these texts reveal to us, as connected with
Baptism, really attend the Baptism of adults; such
adults, of course, coming with due qualifications? Do
you believe, that an *adult* must be born of water, and
of the Spirit, before he can enter into the kingdom of
God?—that when an *adult* comes to Baptism, repenting
and believing, his sins are there and then washed away,
as St Paul's were?—that *so many adults* as are baptized
into Jesus Christ, are baptized into His death, and consequently buried with Him in Baptism? that *so many
adults* as have been baptized into Christ, have put on
Christ?—that *adults* are cleansed from their sins, with
the washing of water, by the word? I think if you
examine the workings of your own mind on the subject,
you will find that it is far more difficult to believe
that the blessings attending Baptism, mentioned in the
texts I have brought forward, are given in the case of
adults than in that of infants. To take a case that
occurred here.—Our former minister baptized some years
ago two grown-up persons. One of them was the son
of Quaker parents, he had lived for some time previous
to his Baptism, a consistent life, and had exhibited many
signs of what is called "true conversion." The other
had been brought up amongst dissenters who denied
Infant Baptism; he also had been for years a regular
attendant at the public service of God, and a man of
unblemished character, but by no means exhibited the
signs of spirituality that the *other* did. The clergyman
wished to put off his Baptism till he should exhibit
more decided marks (as he expressed it) of genuine
religion, but he said, ' what right have you to keep
' me back from an ordinance that our Lord declares
' necessary to salvation? I will unfeignedly renounce
' the Devil and all his works, and I heartily believe

'that Jesus Christ is the Son of God.' They were accordingly both baptized. Now, respecting the first, I felt it most difficult to believe, that, not till the moment of Baptism, (and certainly he was not till then born of water), he was regenerated, and grafted into the body of Christ's Church; but to which must I give credit, the *express* words of my Saviour, or my preconceived notions? "Heaven and earth shall pass away, but MY "word shall not pass away." Respecting the second, it was equally difficult, from opposite reasons, to believe that in his case such great and inconceivable benefits took place, as that he should be co-buried and co-raised with Christ—clothed with Christ,—and receive the remission of his sins; and yet he appeared to be far better qualified for Baptism than many of the Christians to whom St Paul addressed his Epistles, whom he speaks to as carnal, and solemnly warns against falling into gross sin; such as the Corinthians, for instance; and yet to all these Corinthians he said, "Ye are washed, "ye are sanctified, ye are justified in the name of the "Lord Jesus, and by the Spirit of our God." "Know "ye not that your bodies are the temples of the Holy "Ghost?" "Know ye not that your members are the "members of Christ?" "Now ye are the body of "Christ, and members in particular."

D. It is indeed most difficult to believe that in Baptism *even persons duly prepared* receive such benefits.

C. It is most difficult to believe, but on that account is it not to be believed, when Scripture expressly asserts it? Believing heartily *all* God's word is most difficult. I mean exercising a *living* faith in *all* of it. And yet to do so, is part of our state of trial. In a cold and dead state of the Church; now happily passed away, we read of many who could not be brought to believe that salvation is only through the merits of our Redeemer; and now in a different state of things Christian responsibility is assailed even in the religious world, and through the instrumentality of professedly religious persons; and the doctrine of a judgment according to works, though supported by innumerable declarations of Scripture, is cast aside. It may not be difficult for a person in this age to believe that Christ died for our sins, and rose again for our justification, and ascended to intercede for us, yet the same person may by no means exercise a realizing faith in the same Saviour as always present in His Church; "Lo, I am with you alway, even unto the end of the world;" or in the doctrine of the Church being the body of Christ, though St Paul has written very much in his Epistles to explain and apply it.

D. But you are wandering from the point. You have not yet begun to shew that those passages you gave me respecting Baptism, apply to the Baptism of Infants as well as to that of adults.

C. I am coming to that very point: I have made some observations to shew that many of us do not believe that this teaching respecting baptism is applicable to *any* Baptism, under *any* circumstances, in this age of the Church. This is most important, for it shews us that we either believe the Sacrament itself to be changed, that it has worn itself out, so to speak, and has not the efficacy it had when Christ instituted it; or it shews us, that our present views of it are unscripturally meagre and inadequate. Allow me, before we discuss the case of Infants, to ask you—Do you believe that it is right to baptize Infants? and, if you do, may I ask your reason for so believing?

D. I believe that it is right to baptize Infants, because I think that they ought to be dedicated to God from their earliest years.

C. But what reasons have you from Scripture for this practice?

D. I consider that Baptism takes the place of Circumcision, and, as the latter was administered to Infants, so also should the former.

I think also that we have full warrant for baptizing them from our Lord's gracious conduct to infants, when He took them up in His arms, put His hands upon them, blessed them, and said, "Of such is the kingdom of God."

Besides, we continually read of the Apostles baptizing whole households, in which households there must have been some children.

And the very fact of there being no command against it makes it more than probable, that it is God's intention that children should be baptized; especially when we take into account the circumstances under which the New Testament was written. These are the leading Scripture reasons I have for the practice.

C. The usual arguments. Let us see whether your holding these does not naturally and fairly require you to hold something further. I think we shall find that *each of the Scripture reasons you have alleged for Infant Baptism is, when examined, a reason for going a step further, and believing, that each child, at its Baptism, receives the Inward and Spiritual Grace with the outward and visible sign.* What was Circumcision?

D. The rite of admission to the privileges of the Jewish Covenant.

C. What privileges did the Jews receive from their covenant?

D. They had the promised land, the possession of the Scriptures, the ordinances and laws of the Jewish Church, and the Messiah came of one of their families.

C. You have omitted one of the most important. Were they not children of God?

D. I think not; at least, *not as a nation.*

C. You are. mistaken. Turn to *Romans* ix. 3, 4.: "I could wish that myself were accursed from Christ for "my brethren, *my kinsmen according to the flesh;* who "are Israelites, to whom pertaineth the *adoption,* &c." Here, you see, that St Paul tells us "that the adoption "belonged to the Israelites *after the flesh,*" not simply to the "elect remnant" who in all ages served God, but to the men who were then filling up the measure of their iniquities by rejecting Christ; for it is only respecting such as these, that St Paul could have the intense sorrow of heart that he describes himself as suffering. You will find that God addressed the nation as His children from the first, and continued to do so, even in the times of their most grievous rebellion. He tried to win them over to live as His children, and return to their Father's house, on the ground that He had already made all of them His children. So *Exodus* iv. 22.: "Israel is My Son, My first born." And *Isaiah* i. 2.: "I have nourished and brought up *children,* "and they have rebelled against Me." Our Lord also, having evident reference to His brethren after the flesh, says to the Syrophenician woman. "It is not meet to "take the *childrens'* bread, and to cast it to the dogs."

But, to take another view of Jewish privileges. We find that Jehovah addressed the Jewish Church, (not in its best times, but when it had departed from Him as an adulteress from her husband) in terms taken from the marriage union, the closest of human relationships. Look at the first three chapters of Jeremiah, especially chapter ii. 2, 3 : —" Go and cry in the ears of Jerusalem, " saying, thus saith the Lord, I remember thee, the kind- " ness of thy youth, *the love of thine espousals* when thou " wentest after me in the wilderness." *Jeremiah* iii. 14 :— " Turn, O backsliding children, *for I am married to you.*" *Ezekiel* xvi. 8 : —" Now when I passed by thee and " looked upon thee, behold thy time was the time of " love ; and I spread my skirt over thee, and covered thy " nakedness : yea, I swear unto thee, and *entered into a* " *covenant with thee,* saith the Lord God, *and thou becamest* " *Mine."* I feel I can give you but a faint idea of the evidence these chapters afford in confirmation of what I have stated respecting this privilege of the Jewish Church, by reading a verse or two from them. I earnestly request you to peruse them for yourself with a view to the matter.*

Now to whom are such expressions as these, so full of grace and love, applied ? Who are they whom God strives to draw to himself with such cords of long-suffering and tender mercy ? Are they the pious Jews, the elect remnant who had not bowed the knee to Baal ? or are they the nation—the mass of the circumcised, who had yet to be exhorted to put away the foreskin of their hearts, and be no more stiff-necked ? Clearly the latter. These passages lose all their force, if applied to those Jews only who realized their state of grace and responsibility. *They* had kept their marriage covenant with God, and so could not with any degree of propriety be exhorted to return, when, with all their deficiencies, they yet continued under the roof of their husband.

D. But was the time of their Circumcision their introduction to these Covenant-blessings *in all cases ?*

O. God tells us so, when He ordains Circumcision. " This is my covenant, which ye shall keep, between Me and you, and thy seed after thee ; every man-child among you shall be Circumcised." If after the eighth day any Jew was not Circumcised, God's covenant with Abraham

---

* See appendix (A) in which the evidence of Jeremiah and Ezekiel is drawn out in full.

was broken in the case of that particular uncircumcised child. "The uncircumcised man-child, whose flesh of his "foreskin, is not Circumcised, that soul shall be cut off "from His people, he hath broken my covenant." You remember that even Moses narrowly escaped death for neglecting this duty to his child. *Exodus* iv. 24, 25. And it was the introduction to these covenant blessings *in all cases*, for if there were *any* Jews to whom Circumcision was a mere form, conveying no covenant blessings, it surely must have been those, who, in the times of Jeremiah and Ezekiel, revolted from God; and yet we have seen how these very backsliders were invited to repent and return, because of covenant blessings already in time past made over to them.

D. I perfectly see to what your argument leads, or at least to what you would wish it to lead. It is that if a Jew, by circumcising his child, necessarily brought him into a state of privilege and responsibility; a Christian, bringing his child to receive the sacrament of initiation into a better covenant, founded on better promises, must expect much more, in Baptism at the hands of God; and that, as in the one case, *all* Jewish children received the peculiar blessings that fitted them for *their* dispensation, so in the other, *all* Christian children must receive a blessing adapted to fit them for the higher and more glorious kingdom into which they are brought.

C. It is, but I would have you carefully remember that ours is an infinitely higher dispensation than the Jewish. We must not lower our children's baptismal blessing, by supposing, that it is nothing more than the blessing received by a Jewish child at its Circumcision. The benefit received by our children in Baptism must be a benefit corresponding to our better state of things. This is the dispensation of the Spirit, and so (to carry out the analogy) our children must be in some mysterious way, by Baptism, made partakers of God's Spirit. This is borne out by the fact,—that we find St Paul in his Epistles, invariably addresses his converts as partakers of the Spirit, though there is ample proof, from the inspired word, that many among them had only, "a name to live, "and were dead." To take the example of the Corinthians. He warns them against the grossest sins, not by denying that they were partakers of the Spirit, and so exhorting them to seek it, but by assuring them, that they were already possessed of it. "Know ye not that your bodies "are the temples of the Holy Ghost?" "Know ye not "that your members are the members of Christ?" "By "one Spirit are we all baptized into one body." "Now "ye are the body of Christ, and members in particular." 1 *Corinthians* vi. 15—20; xii. 13. 27. I say *invariably*, for we do not find a single instance to the contrary. Nothing can be more marked than the contrast between St Paul's way of speaking to Churches, which, even at that early age, were composed both of good and bad, and that adopted among Christians calling themselves Spiritual at the present day. But the limits of a conversation, like that in which we are now engaged, are utterly inadequate to bring before you the mass of evidence on this subject from the Apostolical Epistles.* *You see then how your first Scripture reason for baptizing infants leads you on to believe that God gives to each Baptized Infant the covenant blessing he has annexed to the Sacrament.*

I will now proceed to consider another reason, taken from Scripture, that you gave for the baptism of Infants. You alluded, I think, to our Lord's laying His hands on them, and blessing them, and saying that "of such is the "kingdom of God;" and you infer, I suppose, from this, that, as our Lord did not then refuse to lay His hands upon them, and bless them, because they could not from their tender years exercise a lively faith in him; so now He will not refuse to receive them in Baptism, though they can no more at the time of their Baptism understand the nature of the rite than those Jewish children could understand what our Saviour Christ meant by His outward gesture and deed. You also infer that if our Lord said of Infants "of such is the kingdom of God," we are by no means to refuse them the sacrament that brings them into that kingdom.

D. I certainly do hold that this act of our Lord is the greatest possible encouragement to a parent to bring his child to Baptism. It removes his chief difficulty, which is the inability of his child, from its tender years,

---

* The reader is particularly requested to peruse appendix (B); in which the evidence on this subject is considered more in full. If he wishes to pursue this branch of Scripture investigation further, he will find the greater part of St Paul's Epistles examined with a view to this subject in my "Second Adam and New Birth," second Edition, chapters vi—xi.

to understand the nature, or appreciate the blessings of our Lord's ordinance.

C. Just so. But must you not go on a step further, and admit that it is not only the greatest encouragement to a parent to bring his child, but also gives him the fullest warrant for believing, that his child *there and then* receives a blessing? If it removes his difficulty respecting the lack of actual faith in his child being a barrier against his receiving Baptism, does it not equally remove the difficulty of believing that his child is, in Baptism, made a member of Christ and the child of God? Let us take this transaction of our Lord's in connection with what he says in other places respecting children. In *St Matthew* xviii. the chapter before the one in which we have this account, we learn, that when the disciples disputed which of them should be the greatest, our Lord "called a little child unto him, and set him in the midst "of them, and said, Verily I say unto you, except ye be "converted, and become as little children, ye shall not "enter into the kingdom of heaven. Whoso shall receive "one such little child in my name, receiveth me. But "whoso shall offend one of these little ones which believe "on me, it were better for him that a mill-stone were "hanged about his neck, and that he were drowned in "the depth of the sea. Take heed that ye despise not "one of these little ones, for I say unto you, that in "heaven their angels do always behold the face of my "Father which is in heaven.........It is not the will of "your Father which is in heaven that one of these little "ones should perish." Can we imagine good-will declared more emphatically than in these expressions? It is saying very little to assert that He puts them on a level with believing adults,—He puts them above them, he holds them forth as an example. Can we believe that He who would thus speak of little children, would either deny them Baptism into His body, or *in any case* degrade their Baptism into a mere form? Is it likely that He who instituted Baptism for the conveyance of such blessings to believing adults, as we have seen in various passages of God's word, should rob it of these blessings in the case of those whom he set forth as patterns of meekness and simplicity to such adults? Every thing that He says of them would lead us to believe, that if He granted them Baptism at all, He would vouchsafe to them its full blessing. If He allowed them to receive it at all, He would ensure that they received it to all the saving intents and purposes for which He instituted it.

D. But can children be said to receive the Sacrament of Baptism worthily when they are conceived and born in sin?

C. Of course no one, strictly speaking, receives it worthily. The best prepared and best qualified adult who receives it, comes to it under the burden of his sins, in order that he may be freed from that burden. At least such was the case with St Paul. To him it was said after he had repented, believed, prayed, and fasted, "Arise, and be baptized, and wash away thy sins." When we speak of receiving it worthily, we mean with due preparation, with the qualifications of sincere repentance and faith, which the Scripture has laid down: and we affirm that what our Lord says of children, "of such is the kingdom of God," fully warrants our believing that God accounts their freedom from actual transgressions and guilelessness in the stead of actual preparation. Each of the children brought to Jesus was, like ours, conceived and born in sin; yet our Lord never alludes to this, but passes it over altogether, and in another place, holds them forth as an example to His followers. He evidently considered that it presented no bar to their receiving His blessing through the laying on of His hands; and this bears us out in believing that Original Sin presents no obstacle to our children receiving grace from Him in a sacrament He has appointed for the conveyance of such grace.

D. But are we warranted in gathering from this transaction that our Lord blesses all infants brought to Him in Baptism, with the grace He has annexed to it? We know that adults can come to Baptism, and from unbelief or carelessness receive no spiritual blessing, and may it not be so with some infants? The case of Simon Magus proves that a person may be baptized, and have neither part nor lot in Christ.

C. There is not one word in the narrative, either in St Matthew, or in the other evangelists, to make us suppose that these children were different from any other children, *i. e.* that they had qualifications for receiving a blessing from the Saviour through the laying on of His hands, which other children had not, and our Lord's words respecting children in the preceding chapter are equally unqualified or unrestricted. Consider the words "Suffer little children to come unto me, for of such is the "kingdom of God." "It is not the will of your Father "which is in heaven that one of these little ones should "perish." Is there any limitation implied here to prevent *any* professing Christian parent from either bringing his child to baptism, or subsequently educating him as one who has then received grace and adoption?

It is impossible to suppose but that each of these children received a blessing, a blessing at the time, which they might afterwards forfeit by actual sin; and yet common sense tells us, that what our Lord did to the infants brought to Him from a particular city, He could not have done to the adults of that city. Why? Because the adults, having a certain freedom of will, must come of themselves; they must have presented themselves to receive imposition of hands, whereas the infants were brought in the arms of others. The adults among whom He sojourned were actuated towards Him by various motives, some by faith, others by unbelief, or curiosity, or malice. It is manifested that if the adults received a blessing from the imposition of His hands, it must be through the co-operation of their own wills, as our Lord only healed those in whom He perceived faith; but not so the children; they were all on a level, they all had to be brought; no one of them repented or believed, any more than another. If birth-sin, or want of reason to understand the rite, could have kept away *one*, or hindered *any* from receiving Christ's blessing, it must have hindered *all*. If guilelessness, or freedom from actual sin was any qualification, all were alike endowed with it. If it is objected that laying on of hands is not baptizing, we reply, that in respect of the adult, it is an act which, equally with Baptism, requires faith to receive either the outward act or the inward benefit, whatever that benefit may be; and consequently the same reasons apply to withholding the one from infants, as the other.

D. But do not many persons belonging to your Church take a different view from the one you do? Do not some say that only those children receive Baptismal grace to whom God has assigned it by a previous decree, and whom He has previously cleansed to render them fit for it? and do not others assert that those children only receive grace, whose parents or sponsors have faith?

C. Would not such principles require our Lord to have spoken and acted very differently from what He did? Would He not on such a view of things have commenced with warning the parents that what they wished for regarding their children was a mere rite or ceremony, efficacious perhaps if there had been a previous decree of His heavenly Father in a particular child's favour, but not without? or He would have bid the parents examine themselves as to the motives wherewith they were bringing their children, and have cautioned them against superstition, and told them that no outward rite, can, in any case, be accompanied with inward blessing, except the recipient be in a fit state of mind; that this was God's unalterable law, and that children formed no exception to it; that as these children were not by nature in a fit state to receive His blessing, being conceived and born in sin, it behoved the parents who brought them, to see to their own faith and holiness, or the children could receive no blessing, as the service would be a mockery. But instead of this, what *does* He say? "Suffer the little children to come unto me, "and forbid them not, for of such is the kingdom of "God." He puts both the parents and their faith entirely out of the question. He does not allude to it, or them, in any way. He does not say, "Suffer the "faithful parents to bring their children," but •He says, "Suffer the little children to come unto me, and forbid "them not, for of such is the kingdom of God." He shews as plainly as both words and deeds can shew, that *children do form an exception to* the rule which some persons put forth as an invariable rule in God's dealings, that none can in any dispensation receive grace, except they are in a fit state of mind at the time, *i. e.* "Unless "they have certain moral pre-requisites such as repent-"ance and faith." As to any previous decree qualifying some children, and disqualifying others, can it by any stretch of interpretation be reconciled with our Lord's express words, "It is not the will of your Father which is "in heaven, that one of these little ones should perish"?

This gracious mode of speaking which our Lord adopts respecting infants, ought, in all fairness, to prevent the misapplication of another passage to their case, the only one of those I enumerated in which Baptismal Grace is spoken of as conditional, 1 *Peter* iii. 21. "The

"like figure whereunto even Baptism doth also now save
"us (not the putting away the filth of the flesh, but
"the answer of a good conscience towards God) by the
"resurrection of Jesus Christ." You hear it said by
those who separate the outward sign from the inward
grace, in the case of Infants, that the answer of a good
conscience is required, or the Baptism is of no saving
efficacy.—Certainly, but to whom does this apply? only
to adults: if it applied to infants, it is equally of force
against their receiving Baptism at all, as their conscience,
not being yet formed, nor capable of discernment, can
give no answer, good or bad. If the infant, when he
grows to man's estate, exhibits no "answer of a good
"conscience towards God," it does not show that he was
not regenerated in Baptism, but it shows that he has
received grace in vain, and must take heed lest he be
in the end found worthy of far sorer punishment, as
one who has "trodden under foot the Son of God, and
"counted the blood of the covenant wherewith he was
"sanctified, an unholy thing, and hath done despite unto
"the Spirit of grace."

The application of the case of Simon Magus to the
Baptism of young children may be answered in the same
manner. Our Lord's mode of speaking of infants, and
His whole demeanour towards them, show that it must
be, to the last degree, contrary to His will, to class
any one of them with that miserable reprobate. *We have
now fully examined the second Scripture reason you gave
for the Baptism of Infants, and we find that it too leads
you on a further step in the same direction; viz. to
assuredly believe that an ever present Saviour gives to
each little one the inward grace with the outward sign.*

D. I grant that the arguments you have brought
forward seem to forbid a separation of the outward
sign from the inward grace of the Sacrament, but I have
several other objections to which I should like to hear
your replies.

C. With all my heart. But before you proceed
to state them, let me call your attention to another
reason you gave for baptizing infants. You mentioned
that the Apostles baptized whole households, and that
it is impossible to suppose but that in these households
there were some children. We have distinct records of
three, viz. of Lydia,—of the Philippian jailor,—and of

Stephanas at Corinth. We naturally gather from this, that, whenever the head of a family embraced the Christian faith, and was baptized, the members of his household were baptized also. At the time, then, that the Apostolical Epistles were addressed to the several churches, there would be in each of those Churches a number of young persons, who had been admitted into the Church in infancy, and growing up, were receiving their profession of faith from their parents just as ours are. Now there is this most remarkable fact to be noticed in these Epistles, that all the Christians of the several Churches to which they were sent, are addressed as being already in a state of grace, and partakers of adoption and of the Spirit of God; and are appealed to, on the strength of this, to "walk worthy of their "vocation," to "quench not the Spirit," and to "work "out a salvation" already commenced. Take for instance St Paul's Epistle to the Romans; The first *practical* application that the Apostle makes of the doctrine of the cross to the hearts, consciences, and lives of the Romans, is in the beginning of the sixth chapter, and is grounded on the fact of the Baptism of each one of them being a burial with Christ, a partaking of the benefits of His death in Baptism; "Know ye not that "so many of us as were baptized into Jesus Christ, "were baptized into His death? Therefore we are "buried with him by Baptism into death; that like as "Christ was raised from the dead by the glory of the "Father, even so we also should walk in newness of life." Could the Apostle have possibly made so general an appeal as this, if he had had the smallest doubt respecting its reaching *all* to whom he wrote? If there were then a number of persons in the Roman Church, concerning whom, on account of their having been baptized in infancy, there were serious doubts as to their having received any thing but the outward form, how could they *all* be addressed as sacramentally dead to sin, and buried with Christ? How could *all* be told to "reckon "themselves dead indeed unto sin, but alive unto God "through Jesus Christ our Lord"? It is worthy of remark that there is not one exhortation to holiness of life in this Epistle, which is not grounded on Baptismal grace; for the Apostle, having devoted his sixth chapter to inculcate holiness, again reverts to doctrinal matters with which he occupies the next five chapters; and when he again resumes the consideration of the duty arising from grace bestowed, at the beginning of the twelfth chapter, he does it by calling to their recollection their Baptismal privilege of being "members of Christ." xii. 4, 5. "For as we have many members in one body, "and all members have not the same office, so we, "being many, are one body in Christ, and every one "members one of another;" and then follows a long series of practical exhortations, all depending on this doctrine of *all* "being one body in Christ." If then the young members of the Roman Church had not, each one for himself, been brought into the body of Christ by Baptism, not one single practical precept, not one motive to a holy life, in the whole Epistle, could be applied to them. We turn to another Epistle, where the same argument of responsibility, arising from grace given in Baptism, is expressed nearly in the same words: *Colossians* ii. 12. iii. 1, 2, 3. "Buried with "Him in Baptism, wherein also ye are risen with Him "through the faith of the operation of God, who hath "raised him from the dead."—"If ye then be risen "with Christ, seek those things which are above, where "Christ sitteth on the right hand of God," "For ye "are dead, &c." Then follow a number of precepts, all deriving their force from this assumed burial of the *Colossians* with Christ in Baptism, and *among them, one to children* (verse 20.), evidently implying what is almost entirely lost sight of, that *they* were baptized, and had each one received in their Baptism not only the outward sign, but the inward grace of a death to sin in Christ. (verse 3.). Let us see what a contrary view would lead to. If, after the example of the Apostles, other missionaries, as converts multiplied, added households to the Church by Baptism, in a few years the proportion of those baptized in infancy would be greatly increased in all the churches. If then, in the case of these baptized as infants, there was no certainty of the inward grace accompanying the outward sign, it could by no means be said to the Galatians in a few years time, "Ye are *all* the children of God by "faith in Christ Jesus, for as many of you as have been "baptized into Christ have put on Christ." The same, of course, may be observed respecting the Corinthians:

the words "Know ye not that your bodies are the
"temples of the Holy Ghost? know ye not that your
"members are the members of Christ?" "By one
"Spirit are we all baptized into one body." "Now ye
"are the body of Christ, and members in particular,"—
would in a few years be to them obsolete forms of
expression, or the occasion of a most dangerous error.
Now, seeing that the Apostle uses the doctrine of
Baptism as one of the strongest motives to his converts
to live holily,—nay, the very strongest, because they
were then united to a holy God and Saviour, by a Holy
Spirit, in order that they might be holy in thought,
word, and deed,—it is a serious thing to think, that
such an appeal could only be made with any shew of
reason within a few years after the first planting of
any Church. Here, too, is *a "first principle of Christ's*
"doctrine," "a foundation," that ceases to be of any
practical utility or extensive application in less than
half a century — ceases to be of any practical utility
when it is most wanted! *We think then that the third*
Scripture reason you gave for Infant Baptism, will, when
examined by the light of other Scripture, lead to a firm
belief in the truth of God's causing the inward grace
to accompany the outward sign in the case of all infants.

D. I cannot but acknowledge the force of much
that you have brought forward; but I must confess
that, though I mentioned several reasons taken from
Scripture in favour of Infant Baptism, my mind often
wavers on the subject. I wish that the evidence for
it in the word of God was more explicit.

C. Very well. If the evidence for Infant Baptism
is insufficient, let us give up the practice, rather than
change, in the case of Infants, that doctrine of the
Sacrament, which we find plainly stated in the word of
God. In the New Testament the grace of Baptism is
declared to be 'remission of sins,' 'a burial and rising
'again with Christ,' 'a putting on of Christ,' and 'a
'grafting into Christ's body.' Let us not separato
what God has joined. If there is good reason from
Scripture for believing that Infants may be baptized,
let them be baptized; let us believe that their Baptism
conveys to each of them the blessings which we have
seen that God has annexed to it, and brings them
under the obligations to holiness which arise from the

fact of their *having received* those blessings; and let us, as we are bound, follow out our belief by plying them with the Baptismal motives to newness of life that we find used in Scripture. You say that you wish the evidence for Infant Baptism was more express than it is. You gave me some short time ago several excellent reasons from Scripture, three of which we have considered at length. I do not see how their force can be evaded.

D. No; but two objections continually present themselves to my mind, and prevent me making that use of the doctrine of the Sacrament which you seem to do; one is, that Infant Baptism is not once mentioned in the New Testament; the other, that the Scriptures seem to imply, that faith is necessary in the recipient, in all cases, before the Sacrament can be administered; so that we have no right to conclude, from the Jews being commanded to Circumcise their children, that we should Baptize ours.

C. I think one consideration drawn from the word of God will enable us to dispose of the latter argument. What is Circumcision called by St Paul in *Romans* iv. 11.?

D. He calls it a seal of the righteousness of the faith which Abraham had being uncircumcised.

C. Here then we have Circumcision described in such a way as apparently to forbid its being administered to any but grown up persons who can exercise faith, and yet we know that when Abraham was circumcised, to whom it was a seal of the righteousness of his previous faith, all his household, including every child above eight days old, was circumcised also. There is no place in the Scriptures where faith is spoken of as requisite for Baptism, more strongly than it is here spoken of as requisite for Circumcision.

Thus then we see that though faith was needful to Abraham before he could receive the sign and seal of God's covenant, yet the want of faith did not hinder the children of his household receiving the same. So in the case of the jailer at Philippi, and of Stephanas at Corinth, though faith was requisite before *they* could be baptized, yet the want of faith did not hinder the children of their households from receiving the same Baptism, as the conveyance to them of the blessings of a more gracious covenant than that which God entered into with Abraham; the Mediator of this new covenant having obviously included children within its scope when He said, "Suffer the little children to come unto Me and "forbid them not, for of such is the kingdom of God"?

D. But it is sometimes objected that we have no evidence that there were children in these households.

C. We read of the Apostles baptizing three households. Now how few records have we in the Acts, and Epistles, of the actual administration of Baptism. We read, *Acts* ii. of the Baptism of three thousand; and enough is written to convince us that if any person, on seeing the miracles of the Apostles, believed, he was baptized; and so the Epistles are addressed to bodies of men, whose Baptism the Apostle takes for granted, though the actual administration of the Sacrament is recorded in but a few instances. As then we must necessarily believe that multitudes were baptized, besides those whose Baptisms are actually recorded; so we must also believe that very many whole households were baptized, besides the three of which particular mention is made. And are we to suppose that in none of these there were any children? Not only must these households have included children, but in accordance with the institutions of society then existing, there must have been slaves, and *their* children, all the absolute property of their master; all of whom would have to be baptized if it could be said, with any degree of correctness, that the *household* was baptized.

D. What you say of Circumcision, as bearing upon Baptism, appears true; but how is it that we are obliged to rely on the Old Testament for so material a part of our argument, when we know that its precepts respecting ritual observances are not binding upon Christians?

C. We Churchmen consider it by no means so material a part of the argument as you do; into this, however, I will not now enter, as I wish to meet you entirely on your own grounds; but remember, that the Old Testament is that part of the word of God which St Paul alludes to when he speaks of "all Scripture "being given by inspiration of God, and profitable for "doctrine, for reproof, for correction, for instruction in "righteousness, that the man of God may be perfect, "throughly furnished unto all good works."

Let me now remind you of another reason you gave for the practice of Infant Baptism, and that is, ' that the ' fact of there being no command against it, makes it more ' than probable that God intended infants to be baptized; ' especially when we take into account the circumstances ' under which the New Testament was written.' Consider who the persons were to whom the first command to receive Christian Baptism was addressed. They were all Jews to whom St Peter said, "Repent, and be baptized "every one of you, in the name of Jesus Christ, for the "remission of sins,"......"for the promise is to you and to "your *children*." How could they understand the words, "and to your children," except as a permission to baptize them? For remember, that they had been educated in a religion, one of the first principles of which was, that children should be admitted into covenant with God from their earliest years. Their education, if it had been a religious one, had been based on the covenant-relation existing between them and the God of Abraham from their eighth day. But a better covenant, founded on better promises, was brought in, which was to supersede the old. And the act of entrance into the grace of the New covenant was a rite, viz. Baptism; just as the act of entrance into the Old was a rite, viz. Circumcision. Baptism, in the one, answering in point of place, to Circumcision, in the other. Would not then these Jewish converts naturally ask, 'are not our children to be ' partakers with us of the blessings of being grafted into ' Christ's body? If we had continued as we were, we ' could have grafted them into God's ancient Church, ' and trained them from the first as partakers of God's ' promise to Abraham, and their Circumcision would have ' been to them an assured token of God's favour. Is ' there to be nothing answering to this in the better state ' of things you are bringing in? Did not your Master ' say respecting little children, "of such is the kingdom ' "of God"? did He not hold them forth as an example ' to adults, and bid us "take heed not to despise one of ' "them"? These considerations will serve to shew, that the earliest converts would naturally expect that their children should be baptized; if therefore such a thing were unlawful, we should look for a plain command against it.

If we are not allowed to baptize our infants, or to believe that Baptism unites them to Christ, and makes them partakers of His death, does it not strike you that the children born under this dispensation of grace, are worse off than the children born under the inferior dispensation that preceded it? We have seen respecting Circumcision, that it at once made the infant a partaker of the blessings and responsibilities of the old covenant; for instance, St Paul says, it made a man "a debtor to "keep the whole law." If we have nothing corresponding to it in our better covenant, then we are driven to the conclusion that motives to holiness could have been addressed to the Jewish child, which cannot now be addressed to the Christian, at least with equal certainty.

For the Jew could say to his child, ' You belong to 'the family of Abraham, the friend of God, and the 'thought of that should make you love God, and hate 'evil. God made a covenant with him, whereby he 'assured to him great and precious promises, and at the 'same time commanded him to walk before Him, and be 'perfect. He made not that covenant with him alone, 'but with all his seed; and so you, from your eighth day, 'have been partaker of the good things of this covenant, 'and have been a child of God, and God has loved you 'as one of the seed of His friend. You have in your 'flesh the very mark God ordained as a pledge of His 'loving kindness to you, and a witness of the way in ' which he requires you to serve Him, by putting away the ' sinful lusts of the flesh. Give yourself up therefore to ' His service who has already brought you near to Himself, ' by having made you His child, a member of His Church, ' and a partaker of all the blessings of His covenant.'

But if we are to give up infant Baptism, or, which is pretty much the same thing, renounce our belief in its saving efficacy *in all cases*, can we similarly appeal to the consciences of our children? Should we not be compelled of necessity to address them as so many heathen children, "having no hope, without God in the world?" We might, it is true, speak of the love of Christ to little children, and so urge them to come to Him; but the Jew would still have an immense advantage over us; he would say, 'God not only loves children,—He loves *you*, and ' has already blessed *you* by bringing you into His cove-'nant:' whereas the Christian could only say, ' God loves

'you if you are one of his elect children. You will know
'by your conversion, whether Christ's ordinance of Bap-
'tism has been anything more than a mere form in your
'case, for then God's Spirit will so act upon you as to
'overpower your will: And till I see the outward signs of
'this work of the Spirit, I cannot hold you responsible
'for any interest in the promises of the Gospel.' *Thus
we see that your fourth Scripture reason for Infant
Baptism equally forbids us to separate the outward sign
from the inward grace in the case of Infants.*

D. I still see some apparently insurmountable difficulties connected with the view of this subject you
advocate.

C. I am most anxious to explain to the best of my
power every difficulty, but remember that the things of
God are so far above our limited understandings, that,
after all our investigations, some difficulties will attend
the most clearly revealed truths. It is part of our trial
to believe the truth in spite of objections, but let us take
especial care that these are not of our own making, by a
too rigid adherence to some human system, contrary in
many important particulars to God's word.

D. My first objection is that, according to your
doctrine, a spiritual effect *necessarily* flows from the
outward administration of the Sacrament.

C. You do not fairly state the case. I am as far as
any one from believing, that there is any inherent virtue
in the Sacrament itself; but I do believe, that God, in
His allwise purposes, has graciously been pleased to
annex a certain grace to the outward sign when that sign
is worthily received; and I do believe that all Infants
receive the Sacrament worthily for reasons I have before
stated. I would put the question in this way. Are
Infants born in sin, inheritors of Adam's evil nature? If
so, is it their fault? Is not this evil nature theirs by the
very fact of their being brought into the world through
the agency of human parents? Is it not clear then that,
at a time when they are perfectly unconscious of what
they are receiving, the evil nature of the first Adam is
communicated to them: they are engrafted into a bad
stock, by an act of others, with which they have nothing
to do? If then, by that of which they are at the time
quite unconscious, viz. their being brought into existence,
they are made partakers of sin and death, (for St Paul

says, *Ephesians* ii. that "all are by nature children of wrath,") why should they not by an act of which they are as little conscious at the time, viz. their Baptism, be made partakers of the righteousness and life of the Second Adam? It must be so, for the Scriptures say, "Where "sin abounded, grace did much more abound." Read all the latter part of the fifth chapter of St Paul's Epistle to the Romans. The Apostle alludes to Infants in verse 14. "Nevertheless death reigned from Adam to "Moses, even over them that had not sinned after the "similitude of Adam's transgression, who is the figure of "him that was to come. But not as the offence, so also "is the free gift.—For if through the offence of one, many "be dead, (*Infants of course as well as adults*) much "more the grace of God, and the gift by grace, which is "by one man, Jesus Christ, hath abounded unto many. "Therefore, as by the offence of one, judgment came "upon all men to condemnation; even so by the right- "eousness of one, the free gift came upon all men to "justification of life." Let us apply these words to the case we are upon. Just as the sin of the first Adam was sufficient to involve a world in ruin, so the righteousness of the Second Adam is sufficient to rescue a world from that ruin. If then for every Infant that comes into the world, inheriting a depraved nature, and defiled by birth-sin, a redemption has been wrought out on the cross of Jesus Christ amply sufficient to atone for its birth-sin; why should not Baptism, applying the blood shed for all men, be given to each Infant, seeing that this blood was shed for it, just as much as for the grown up sinner who comes to Baptism with the clearest views of its nature and obligations? It received a curse, as a child of the first Adam, why should it not similarly, *i. e.* when unconscious at the time, receive a blessing in a dispensation where "grace much more abounds" under the Second Adam? This chapter (v.) of St Paul's Epistle to the Romans prepares my mind to believe and expect, that God will at least accord to His Son Jesus Christ, the Second Adam, what he accorded to the first Adam. Now God accorded to the first Adam, that mankind through him should receive a taint of sin, and an entailed condemnation from their very birth—that the helpless Infants of his posterity should be made sinners from the womb, by having his sin imputed to them by the very fact of their parents bringing them into existence. And all, without exception, are thus begotten in sin. Why then may I not believe, that God who is *rich* in mercy, will contrive a way by which helpless Infants may have the righteousness of the Second Adam imputed, and His Spirit imparted to them when they are unconscious of what they are receiving? And this must apply to all children, in order that, at least in the Gospel kingdom, the remedy may be co-extensive with the disease.

Of course we are referring to the children of professing Christian parents only, for we do not baptize indiscriminately the children of the heathen, because we know for a certainty that they will not be brought up in the knowledge of their privilege, and so the Sacrament will be, to all intents and purposes, thrown away.

D. Are there not, however, certain expressions in the first Epistle General of St John that appear to militate against your view of the Regeneration of all Infants in Baptism? I think you must allow—indeed the thing is too evident to be contradicted for a moment— that the vast majority of those baptized in infancy fall into many and grievous sins, and can by no means be said to love their brethren with a Christian love, and they are overcome by the world; and yet St John tells us, "Whosoever is born of God doth not commit sin:" "We know that we have passed from death unto life, "because we love the brethren:" "Whatsoever is born "of God overcometh the world." How do you reconcile strong statements such as these with your view of Regeneration.

C. Let me first ask,—how do you reconcile them with *your* view of Regeneration? You hold that Regeneration is that total change of heart and mind, of views, feelings, affections, and desires, which I denominate Renewal or Conversion: this, you assert, is "to be born "again;" and the Apostle says, "Whosoever is born of "God doth not commit sin." Now I ask you to call to mind the most perfect Christian you ever knew, and tell me, would not that man confess with the same St John, "If we say that we have no sin, we deceive ourselves, and "the truth is not in us;" and with St James, "In many "things we offend all;" and with truth too, and yet would you deny him spiritual Regeneration in *your* sense of the word? Again, when you look at the history of the

Church from the time of the Apostles to the present, and see how men who were *in the main* good men and good Christians, exhibiting decided marks of what you call spiritual enlightenment, have yet disputed one among another to the subversion, *for the time,* of Christian charity; would it not require a very bold figure of speech to say, that they *loved the brethren,* i. e. the particular brethren they were opposed to? And ask any minister of the Gospel you choose, whether he has not known, and mourned over, persons who exhibited at one time every mark of being 'savingly influenced by the Spirit,' and yet afterwards entangled in, and overcome by the world.

2 *D.* Undoubtedly what you say is true, and all are alike agreed that the words of the Apostle cannot be taken absolutely in their bare literal meaning. Do not you think we may explain them thus, " Whosoever is " born of God doth not *habitually* commit sin." " They " that are born of God, *generally speaking,* love the " brethren. " Whatsoever is born of God, *eventually* " overcometh the world."

C. No, I do not think such explanation satisfactory, for by it you make one Apostle contradict another: you make St John contradict both St Paul, and St Peter. All the Epistles were written in the same age of the Church to men exposed to nearly the same dangers, and temptations. We may take it for granted, that St John addressed his *general* Epistle to such persons as those to whom St Paul addressed his *particular* Epistles. Now let us bear in mind one circumstance connected with the early churches. They were harassed by a class of Heretics called Gnostics, who, amongst other wicked errors, denied the truth of our Lord's human nature,—that is, that He was man like ourselves in all things, sin excepted; they also denied that He was the Christ; and introduced the most shameless Antinomianism, asserting that a Christian had full liberty to commit what sins he pleased. To these persons the Apostles are continually alluding, and St John especially, from the very best authority (that of Irenæus), is known to have written his Epistle with the view of combating these errors. On this account he says, "Every spirit that confesseth not that Jesus Christ is " come in the flesh, is not of God;" which he says

in order to oppose their false doctrine respecting our
Lord's nature; and further, " Who is a liar but he
" that denieth that Jesus is the Christ ? " an assertion
made in opposition to the same heretics who affirmed
that the Son of God, and the Christ, were different
persons. I mention these texts to show clearly that
his Epistle was mainly written to confute the Gnostics,
or he could not have introduced such expressions. He
had, however, to oppose their deadly Antinomianism also.
They asserted that a man's being born of God gave
him a license to sin with impunity, and to conform to
heathenism rather than endure persecution for Christ.
Against this, his argument is of this sort—' You mistake
' Christianity altogether. It is a holy, self-denying,
' unworldly principle, whereas you make it a carnal and
' a worldly one. Whosoever is born of God doth not
' commit sin *in so far as he is born of God*. The principle
' given him at the time of his new birth was a holy
' principle, opposed to sin, for it was the influence of
' the Holy Spirit of God. When allowed its *full* effect in
' the soul it will extirpate all sin, fill a man with love
' to God, and to his brother, and enable him to overcome
' the world. The Christian who commits sin does not
' commit it as having liberty to do so by virtue of
' being born of God, but he sins at the instigation of
' the evil nature remaining in him from his first birth.
' The Christian, who is, in the very least degree, overcome
' by the world, is overcome *in spite of* the new principle
' implanted in him—in the face of his new birth, not
' in accordance with it, as you Gnostics affirm.*—
' In this way St John's mode of speaking exactly
' agrees with St Paul's in *Romans* chap. vi. where the
latter appeals to them against similar Antinomianism,

---

* The writer desires to direct the attention to the following
quotation from St Augustine as exactly expressing his views of the
true interpretation of this passage. " He that is born of God sinneth
" not." " For were this nativity by itself alone in us, no man would
" sin: and when it shall be alone, no man will sin. But now we
" as yet drag on that which we were born corruptible, although
" according to that which we are new born, *if we walk aright*, from
" day to day we are renewed inwardly. But when this corruptible
" shall have put on incorruption, life will swallow it up wholly, and
" not a sting of death shall remain, now this sting of death is sin."
St Augustine contra Mendacium.

on the ground of each one of the Roman converts "being "buried with Christ in Baptism," *to the end that* they should " walk in newness of life." If any of the Romans continued in sin, it did not make void the Apostle's words, that they were in Baptism united to Christ, and partakers of his death; but it shewed that they went counter to the principle, the intention, and the grace of their Baptism. So when St John says, " Whosoever is born of God doth not commit sin," he cannot mean to contradict what he had said a little before, " If we say that we have no sin, we deceive ourselves; " he must mean, whenever a Christian commits sin, he acts in direct opposition to the principle of his new birth. Again, the same Spirit who inspired St John to write his General Epistle, inspired St Paul to write his Epistle to the Corinthians, in which the latter had to combat the very same three evils that St John had to oppose in his. St Paul had to warn and admonish those, who, so far from " not committing sin," were falling into the deadly sin of fornication (1 *Cor.* v. 1—7. vi. 18. x. 8.); he had to admonish those who, so far from " loving the brethren," were, by reason of their envying, strife, and divisions, yet carnal (1 *Cor.* iii. 3.); he had to admonish those who, so far from " overcoming the world," were conforming to heathen practices (1 *Cor.* viii. x. 7. 14. 21.). And what arguments does he employ? Does he deny their *regeneration* in the case of those who fell? No, he appeals to them upon it in the words, "Know ye not that ye are the temple of God?" "Know ye not that your members are the members "of Christ?" Know ye not that your body is the "temple of the Holy Ghost *which is in you?*" "Ye "are washed, ye are sanctified, ye are justified in the "name of the Lord Jesus, and by the Spirit of our God." "By one Spirit are we *all* baptized into one body." "Now ye are the body of Christ, and members in "particular." "We then, as workers together with Him "beseech you, that ye *receive not the grace of God in* "*vain.*" (1 *Cor.* iii. 16. vi. 15. 19; xii. 13. 27.; 2 *Cor.* vi. 1.) I think you will see by this, that no other interpretation of St John than that I have mentioned, will make him speak the same thing as St Paul. And similarly with what we shall advance from St Peter.

If St John, by saying " Whatsoever is born of God
" overcometh the world," means that God grants to every
one, once regenerate, infallible perseverance to eternal life,
how could St Peter with any truth speak of persons who,
" having *escaped* the pollutions of the world *through*
" *the knowledge of the Lord and Saviour Jesus Christ*,
" are again entangled therein, and overcome, and so
" the latter end is worse with them than the beginning."
But the agreement of St John with both his brother
Apostles will be abundantly manifest, if we understand
him to mean by the expression, " Whatsoever is born
" of God overcometh the world," that the new principle
implanted in a Christian at his Baptism, will, *in so
far* as it is influential, and is allowed full scope, infallibly
overcome the world; and that he uses this argument
in opposition to those heretics who maintained that a
man, by virtue of his new birth, is at liberty to conform
to the world.

Again, supposing that St John is writing to the same
sort of Churches as those to whom St Paul wrote *his*
Epistles, he must write to some who were not exhibiting
signs of Regeneration, but rather the contrary. On *your*
principles, how inconceivable it is that he does not exhort his readers to become regenerate. On *our* principles
such an extraordinary omission is quite consistent; he
considers them by Baptism regenerate, and exhorts them
to let that Spirit which they had received work its full
work within them; in the same way as St Paul, who does
not exhort the Corinthians to become temples of the
Spirit, but to live as men who were already made His
temples.

D. Do not St Peter and St James, in their respective
Epistles, tell us, that *the word of God* is sometimes the
instrument of our Regeneration, apart from Baptism?
Does not St Peter say " being born again not of corruptible
" seed, but of incorruptible, by the word of God;" and
St James, " of his own will, begat He us with the word
" of truth," without mentioning Baptism?

C. No. If their words imply what you seem to think
they do, they would contradict our Lord's words, " Except
" a man be born of *water* and of the Spirit, he cannot
" enter into the kingdom of God." Where do they use
such an expression as " we are born of the word without

"Baptism"[*] The Apostles Peter and James do not allude in these passages to the written or preached word merely, but to the whole Gospel dispensation, under which are included all the means which contribute, in the various ways God has appointed, to bring about man's new birth in Baptism. Under this dispensation is included, first and above all, the gift of the incarnate Word, into whose mystical body we are grafted when baptized; then the written or preached word, by which the conscience of the adult sinner is awakened, and he is led to seek Baptism, then the word of Institution coupled with the word of promise of the Saviour (*Matthew* xxviii. 19, 20.) to be with his Church to the end of the world, and so to make the Baptism of its least minister, in its latest age, as valid and efficacious as that of an Apostle, and by which word each administration of Baptism becomes His act, not the act of the Baptizer; Baptism not being a mere bath or washing, but a bath or washing in the name of the Father, and of the Son, and of the Holy Ghost.

D. I am ashamed to mention another objection, grounded on a passage of Scripture, still it is so often used that I should like to hear your answer to it. Persons say it is utterly incredible that St Paul could

---

[*] But supposing that they do allude to the power of the written or preached word on the conscience, a familiar case will shew that by this they did *not* mean to exclude our Lord's ordinance.—A missionary goes to Hindostan to preach the word of God. A Hindoo by the grace of God feels the power of that word, is convinced of his sin, of his need of a Saviour, and that Jesus Christ is such a Saviour as he needs. He is converted, and baptized. Three things contribute to his new Birth: *First*, the will of God which brought the missionary to his abode; *Secondly*, the word of God which, under grace, convinced his conscience; *Thirdly*, the Saviour's Sacrament, in which he was born of water and the Spirit, and so entered into the kingdom of God. Well; the same Hindoo is encouraged by the missionary to bring his Infant to baptism, by which it too is born again by the same means as its father was: *First*, by the will of God which brought the missionary: *Secondly*, by the word of God, in such texts as "Suffer the little children to come unto me, and forbid them not, "for of such is the kingdom of God." "Take heed that ye despise "not one of these little ones," &c.; which texts encouraged its father to bring it, by Baptism, to Christ, as well as the missionary to receive it in Christ's name. *Thirdly*, by the act of Baptism, as its father was. If it be objected that the child cannot be in Baptism, born "by the "word," because it neither understands nor has faith in that Word, I answer, that this equally tells against its being baptized till it has the full use of reason.

have believed that Baptism conveyed regeneration, when he thanks God that he baptized none of the Corinthians but Crispus and Gaius, and that "God sent him not "to baptize, but to preach the Gospel." (1 *Corinth.* i. 14. 17.).

C. I am glad you are ashamed of such an objection. It is incredible to me how any man, after reading the whole chapter containing this text, could use such an argument, St Paul gives the reason *why* he thanks God that he had baptized only two of the Corinthians, in the very next verse. And what is that reason? "He "thanked God that he had baptized none of them "*lest any man should say that he had baptized in his* "OWN *name.*" The Corinthians were divided into parties. One said, I am of "Paul;" another, "I am of Apollos." If St Paul had baptized many of the Corinthians, those who had been baptized by him would have boasted that they were baptized by one who was not a whit behind the chiefest Apostles, whereas those baptized by Apollos, they would affirm, had only been baptized by an inferior minister: and so Christ's holy ordinance, "the one Baptism," would have been the occasion of division instead of union. St Paul thanks God that he has given no occasion for division; inasmuch as the baptism of Apollos, or any other minister commissioned to perform it, was as valid for uniting a man with Christ in His death, and grafting him into Christ's body, and making him put on Christ, as that of the highest Apostle in the Church. Your argument would be excellent if any one in the Church affirmed, that the grace of Baptism was in proportion to the dignity of the administrator,—that an Archbishop's Baptism conveyed more grace than a Bishops's—a Bishop's Baptism more than a parish priest's;—but if that argument be used for the purpose of making St Paul disparage his Master's ordinance, and contradict himself, it only shews the ignorance or dishonesty of the man who uses it;—his ignorance, in being unacquainted with the context,—his dishonesty in passing such an interpretation on his hearer's, or reader's credulity, in the confident expectation that they would not refer to the context.

The inconsistency of persons who use this argument is still more glaring, when we consider that they allow that Baptïsm conveys spiritual blessings to believing adults, and that the majority of those baptized in the Apostle's time were sincere in their profession. Surely, in the case of *such* persons as St Paul's converts, it could not have been a form so insignificant as to make the Apostle thank God that he was not troubled with the administration of it.

I repeat again, I am glad you are ashamed of such an objection.

D. As you encourage me to mention any objections that may present themselves on this subject, I am sure you will bear with me while I bring under your notice some few others, which I am frequently in the habit of hearing.

C. Bring forward all you remember. I know, from my own experience, how often an objection, to which one does not readily see the answer, will weigh against the clearest evidence of an important doctrine; and hinder us from making that profitable use of it which God intends, by destroying, or weakening our faith in such doctrine.

D. Well then, there is a passage in the second chapter of St Paul's Epistle to the Romans, which clearly implies that no outward rite is of any avail, unless there be a changed heart and a right life on the part of him who has received it. " He is not a Jew, which "is one outwardly; neither is that Circumcision, which "is outward in the flesh: But he is a Jew, which is one "inwardly; and Circumcision is that of the heart, in the "Spirit, and not in the letter; whose praise is not of "men, but of God." May we not say the same of the Christian profession and Baptism, that 'he is not a 'Christian, which is one outwardly; neither is that 'Baptism, which is outward in the flesh, &c.' ?

C. Assuredly we must say so, but then we must take heed that we say it in the same sense as St Paul said what he did of Circumcision; not in a sense which his words will never admit of, when duly considered.

First then, let me ask, does St Paul mean, when he says, "he is not a Jew that is one outwardly," that when a descendant of Abraham did not lead the life that he was bound to do by his profession, he was on that account not a Jew by nation, but belonged to some other race? He certainly cannot mean that.

Again, does St Paul mean, that the cutting of his flesh, which every Israelite underwent on his eighth day, was not literally Circumcision? Certainly not; for that was the name that was given to the outward rite by God himself (*Genesis* xvii. 10, 11.) Again, does St Paul mean that this outward rite did not bring the child into covenant with God? He cannot mean this, for God said, when he instituted Circumcision, "My covenant shall be *in your flesh* for an everlasting "covenant." Again, does St Paul mean that the outward rite did not bring a man under Responsibility? He could not mean that either, for he himself says in another place (*Gal.* v. 2.), "I testify again to *every* "*man* that is circumcised, that he is a debtor to keep the whole law." He must mean the same as what he had indicated a few verses before, that Circumcision is not only a rite, but a state, into which a man is brought by the rite; a state which, by disobedience, may be made uncircumcision, without implying for a moment that the man was not originally circumcised, — or that his Circumcision was not the token of a covenant made at the time on God's part, — or that the covenant sign did not bring him under an obligation to keep the whole law. In this way we may apply this text to Baptism. We must tell the baptized man, living in sin, that his Baptism profits him nothing; nay rather, will immeasurably increase his condemnation, but this is a very different thing from telling him that his Baptism *was nothing*. It would be well for him if it was. That he is not now "walking in newness of life," does not prove that he was not once "buried with Christ in Baptism," in order that he *might* "walk in newness of "life." The Corinthians were many of them defiling the body of Christ, but St Paul does not rebuke their various sins by denying that they had been made partakers of the Spirit in Baptism. On the contrary, he says to them, "By one Spirit are we all baptized into one "body."—"Now ye are the body of Christ, and members "in particular."

D. There is another passage of which a similar use is made in *Galatians* vi. "In Christ Jesus neither "Circumcision availeth anything, nor uncircumcision, but "a new creature."

C. Ask the persons who bring forward this text,

if they dare to substitute the word "Baptism" for the word "Circumcision," and say, 'In Christ Jesus neither 'Baptism availeth anything, nor the neglect of Baptism, 'but a new creature,'—If they dare to assert, that the Baptism, which Christ instituted in His last words on earth, and His Apostles preached for remission of sins, and putting on of Christ, is so utterly useless a ceremony, that it is of no consequence whether a follower of Christ despises it, or not. If they dare not say such a thing, why do they bring forward the passage? If they say they do so to warn the Baptized that their Baptism will not avail unless they live as "new creatures in Christ," we reply, that we go much further, and say, that so far from it availing, it will be the means of treasuring up against them *far more* wrath in the day of wrath and revelation of the righteous judgment of God.

D. Another text to which frequent reference is made is 2 *Corinthians* v. 17. "If any man be in Christ, "he is a new creature; old things are passed away; "behold, all things are become new." The signs of the new creature are laid down, such as new hopes, new affections, new desires, new fears; and it is asserted that if any man have not these marks, *i. e.* is not a truly converted man, he is not in Christ, and never has been; his Baptism was nothing but a mere form, which did not graft him into Christ, or make him partaker of the Spirit.

C. To make the text mean all this, it must be considerably altered, and must be read, 'If any man 'be once in Christ, he will always continue to abide 'in Him as a new creature;' whereas our Lord said, "Every branch IN ME that beareth not fruit God "taketh away"; and counselled His very Apostles to abide in Him; warned them, that if they did not abide in Him, they would not bear fruit; and told them how they were to abide in Him, viz. "by keeping His commandments." (*St John* xv. 1—6.). Every word of this implies that they would not *necessarily* abide in Him because they had been once grafted into His body. I believe that every infant is made, at its Baptism, a new creature, *as far as its circumstances will admit;* the guilt of its birth sin, derived from the old Adam, is washed away; it is brought into a new state; grafted into a new stock; has a new relationship to God given it;

and is endowed with a new principle, which, *if duly improved*, will enable it, *but not compel it*, to walk in newness of life: but its Baptism does not place it in new circumstances of life; it does not give it, for instance, religious parents, who will tenderly foster the grace given it; and will not keep it out of the way of vicious associates. If its parents were ungodly before its Baptism, they will be so after, and being averse to holiness themselves, they are not likely to bring up a child as if it were "*holy*," (1 *Corinthians* vii. 14.) If the parents, though religious persons when they brought their child to the font, had inadequate views of the Sacrament of Baptism, through adherence to a false system, its Baptism will not change *their* deeply rooted prejudices, and make them look for, and tenderly cherish, a principle of grace which they conscientiously think it presumptuous to expect.

This reminds me of another objection brought by unthinking people against the Church doctrine of the Regeneration of all infants duly baptized. We are asked how we can suppose it possible that all the professing Christians belonging to corrupt Churches, (such as those of the Roman Catholic and Greek Communions), are regenerated in Baptism, when they for the most part grow up in such abject superstition and ignorance. We answer, that regeneration is only the beginning of a life which has to be nourished by food adapted to it. This food is the word of God, and the ordinances of His Church. If the word of God is withheld, and the ordinances of His Church debased by idolatrous additions to their primitive simplicity, the child must of necessity grow up ignorant and superstitious. It is the word of God that witnesses of the Saviour, converts the soul, gives wisdom to the simple, rejoices the heart, gives light to the eyes; in a word, makes the man of God perfect, throughly furnished unto all good works. If this word of God is withheld, the soul, humanly speaking, must suffer. The Baptism of an infant in Spain or Italy does not give to his parents or sponsors a knowledge of God's word, neither does it bring him into a state of religious liberty in which he can, without molestation, read it, or hear it read in his own tongue; it does not give him spiritual instructors capable of applying it to his conscience. It does not remove from the Church he frequents the images before which he is taught to bend his knees, nor does it insert the second commandment into the catechism he is taught to repeat, from which catechism it has been designedly excluded. Why then are we to believe that God's sacrament is deprived of its grace because men hinder its blessed effects by their ignorance and superstition?

D. But when you look at the state of professing Christians, and see how some are blinded by ignorance; others enslaved by superstition; so few, even in the most favoured parts of God's vineyard, living to Him; so many fulfilling the desires of the flesh and mind:—do you not feel it sometimes very hard to believe that all these were, in Baptism, brought into a state of salvation, and made partakers of God's Spirit?

C. I should feel it hard had not God's word fully prepared me to look for such a state of things; but so much is written in my Bible to lead me to expect it, that I have no difficulty whatever. That the vast mass of professing Christians should be brought into a state of salvation only to neglect it, and receive God's Spirit only to grieve and quench that Spirit, appears to me the fulfilment of Prophecy.

I look into the Old Testament. I find it taken up with the history of a people whom God brought so near to Himself as to call them His children, His bride, His peculiar people, and yet at no period did any, but a very small remnant, cleave to Him. They set up their idol temples close to the house where He was visibly present by the Shechinah above the Mercy Seat. Yet when He exhorts them to put away their abominations and return to Him, He appeals to them on the ground of *their being in covenant with Himself, His children, His bride; (Isaiah* i. *Jeremiah* ii. iii. *Ezekiel* xvi.) They were brought by a miracle out of Egypt, fed supernaturally with manna, guided through all their journeyings by the angel of His presence in a pillar of cloud and of fire, and yet "their carcasses fell in "the wilderness because of unbelief." From first to last God's dealings with them, and their returns of gratitude, may be summed up in the words, "What could "have been done more to my vineyard that I have "not done in it? wherefore, when I looked that it should "bring forth grapes, brought it forth wild grapes?"

Thus was it with the Church of the Old Covenant.
I confess to you that, had I not the New Testament,
I should never have supposed that such a state of things
could have occurred under the better covenant, when the
Son of God had taken upon Himself our nature, and
suffered death to atone for sin, and taken our nature up
to heaven, and sent down the Third Person of the Trinity
to dwell in men and baptize them into His body, in order
that His Church should be brought into such close union
with Him as to be one with Him, bone of His bone, flesh
of His flesh. I should certainly have expected that every
member of such a Church, so glorified with grace and
privilege, would be perfectly holy. I should never have
thought human nature capable of receiving *such* grace in
vain; counting *such* precious blood with which they had
been sanctified, unholy; and resisting, quenching, doing
despite to, *such* a Spirit. But when I turn to the New
Testament, I find in the first place that, even before His
Church was set up, our Lord prophesied concerning it,
that it would be a mixed Church. He compared it to a
vine having both fruitful and unfruitful, and even withered
branches; a field sown with wheat and tares, both to
grow together till the harvest; a net enclosing good and
bad fish, waiting their final separation at His coming.

I look further, and I find this His prophecy fulfilled
even in the times of the Apostles. I find these Apostles,
in the best and purest age of the Church, warning their
converts by the very example of the children of Israel resisting God, disobeying his calls, and miserably perishing,
(1 *Corinth.* x. 1—14; *Hebrews* iii. 7—19; iv. 1, 2. 11;
Jude 5.). These same converts are *all* addressed as *buried
and risen with Christ in Baptism,* (*Rom.* vi. 4.; *Coloss.* ii.
12.); *clothed with Christ therein.* (*Gal.* iii. 27.); *washed
with the washing of Regeneration in Baptism* (*Ephes.* v. 26;
Titus iii. 5.); *made members of Christ by the Spirit*
(1 *Corinth.* xii. 13. 27., also vi. 15. 19; *Rom.* xii. 4, 5;
Ephes. v, 29, 30, 31, 32, 33; *Coloss.* i. 24. 27, 28); *made
partakers of the same Spirit* (1 *Corinth.* vi. 19; 1 *Thess.*
iv. 7, 8.). And yet with all this, there is scarcely an
Epistle which does not sorrowfully imply, that some
among those to whom it was written might be *falling from
grace* (*Gal.* iii. 1; v. 4.); *quenching the Spirit* (1 *Thess.*
v. 19.); *receiving grace in vain* (2 *Corinth.* vi. 1.);
glorying in their shame (*Phil.* iii. 19.); *committing deadly*

sin (*Ephes.* v. 1—15; *Coloss.* iii. 5, 6.); *selling their birthright* (*Heb.* xii. 14, 15, 16, 17.); *deceiving their own souls by* " *hearing without doing* " (*James* i. 22.) ; *falling from their own steadfastness* (2 *Peter* iii. 17.).

If then Churches, gathered out and ruled over by Apostles, kept pure from within, as far as could be, by wholesome discipline, from without, by fiery trials and persecutions, had each an increasing number of unsound members ; are we not led to expect that such will be the case, to a far greater extent when ordinary ministers preach, and discipline is relaxed, and the world favours the Church, and it is even discreditable not to make some profession of religion ?

Does the alteration in the circumstances of the Church allow us to change the Apostle's doctrine of Baptism, and to cast aside the Apostle's motive to holiness ; a motive grounded on the fact of all having received grace in Baptism ? We think not ; for the mixed state of the Church, the only reason that is alleged as an excuse for so doing, applies equally to the times of the Apostles as to our own. If it is wrong now to beseech *all* the Baptized not to receive God's grace in vain, nor to defile the members of Christ, because the carnal and careless are the large majority, was it not equally wrong when they were (as we hope) the minority ?

D. You have said enough to shew me that the proportion between the godly and ungodly in the Church does not affect the question. The difficulty is, that any human being can be, *at one time,* so in the favour of God as to be called His son, and at another time, cast away for ever for disobedience.

C. Just so ; that is the difficulty ; but then it is one which the word of God itself has met, and answered. I need only remind you of the "angels that kept not their first estate ;" *they* must have been once high in God's favour, and yet they are now " reserved in chains under "darkness unto the judgment of the great day." *And the Apostle Jude puts Christians in remembrance of their doom.* Remember our first parents too, what a state of favour they fell from ! and the Israelites in all stages of their history, and the primitive Christians who were adorned with such glorious titles, and yet bid to take heed after the example of the Israelites. Think of that remarkable passage in the Psalms, alluded to by our Lord

himself, "I have said ye *are God's*: and *all of you* are
"*children of the Most High;* But ye shall die like men,
"and fall like one of the princes." (*Ps.* lxxxii. 6, 7.).
Think too of *Hebrews* xii. 22. "Ye are come unto Mount
"Sion, and unto the city of the Living God, the heavenly
"Jerusalem, and to an innumerable company of angels,
"to the general assembly and Church of the first-born,
"which are written in heaven, and to God the Judge of
"all, and to the Spirits of just men made perfect, and to
"Jesus the Mediator of the New Covenant, and to the
"blood of sprinkling, that speaketh better things than
"that of Abel." Surely you would say that they, who
had come to such and so great things, must be already in
the regions of the blessed, already safe in the glorious
abode into which sin cannot enter: but how does the
Apostle go on? "*See that ye refuse not him that speaketh.*
"For if they escape not who refused him that spake
"on earth; much more shall not we escape, if we turn
"away from Him that speaketh from heaven." Could
words be found in the whole compass of human language
to express more strongly, that men may be in the highest
state of grace, and yet have good reason to take heed
lest they fall away?*

D. Is it not often said that the doctrine of Baptismal Regeneration has a direct tendency to keep the
soul in a state of Spiritual death; to make it self-satisfied
whilst living in conformity with the world; and fatally to
deceive the mass of professing Christians, manifestly not
living to God, by allowing them to think that they can
enjoy heaven without a complete change of heart and
life?

C. I trust I have already said enough to shew you
the falsehood of ascribing such effects to the teaching of
this truth. How does St Paul use the doctrine of ·
Baptism? In the passage I have so frequently alluded
to (*Romans* vi.), so far from considering that it has a
tendency to keep the soul in a state of Spiritual death, he
urges on the Romans the grace of union with Christ,
received at their Baptism, as the strongest obligation on

---

* The reader will find the whole question of Election and Final
Perseverance, and its bearing on Baptismal Grace, examined in the
"Second Adam and New Birth," chapters xv. xviii. and Appendix
C. Third edition. Bell and Daldy.

each one of them to "walk in newness of life;"— to
"reckon themselves dead indeed unto sin, but alive unto
"God through Jesus Christ our Lord." Similarly in
Colossians (ii. iii.), he appeals to those who were buried
and risen with Christ in Baptism to "seek those things
"which are above, where Christ sitteth on the right hand
"of God," and to "set their affections on things above,
"not on things on the earth." As I shewed before at
large, he bids the Corinthians "take heed," by a similar
reference to their Baptismal deliverance. Every call to
holiness of life, every warning against sin, is addressed
equally to every convert, and is grounded on the fact of
each one being a partaker of grace received in Baptism,
as well as couched in such language, that, if he were not
a partaker of such Baptismal grace, the call or warning
could not be addressed to him.

If those who preach the Church's doctrine were in
the habit of asserting, or implying in their teaching, as
some do, in the teeth of all Scripture, that a man *once* in
grace is *always* in grace, there might be some ground for
the charge you mention;—but if they state that Baptism
brings a man into a state of salvation, which state has to
be "worked out with fear and trembling";—if they tell
him that, though grafted into Christ in Baptism, he must
abide in Him, or be in danger of being cast forth by the
Almighty husbandman, as a withered branch;—if they
address the baptized as St Paul did, "We then, as
"workers together with him, beseech you also that yo
"receive not the grace of God in vain;"— if they tell
them, as they are bound to do, that they must "hold fast
"their profession," or they will be in danger of far sorer
punishment, as those "who have counted the blood of
"the covenant, wherewith they were sanctified, an unholy
"thing, and have done despite unto the Spirit of grace;"—
if, I say, they do this, I cannot see but that they are free
"from the blood of all men;" and not only so, I must
go further, and say, that if the mode of speaking used
in the Apostolical Epistles is to be any rule for ministers
in this age of the Church, none but those, who habitually
address *all their baptized hearers as answerable for grace
given,* can be free from their blood. Judge for yourself;
which doctrine is most likely to be perverted to the soul's
destruction? Which chimes in most readily with the
wish to indulge here to the full the desires of the flesh

and mind, and yet at last attain to heaven; the Church doctrine which says to the sinner —'You *have already* 'been brought into a state of salvation which you must 'work out with fear and trembling, or you will assuredly 'fall from it, and your last state will be worse than 'the first. You *have been* delivered from the power of 'darkness, and translated into the kingdom of God's dear 'Son. Remember that Lot's wife, having been saved 'from the destruction of Sodom, yet perished miserably. 'You *have been saved;* remember that God, having saved 'the people out of the land of Egypt, afterward destroyed 'them that believed not. You *are already* a partaker in 'some mysterious way of the Spirit, grieve Him not, or at 'last you may quench Him, and have never forgiveness; 'you *are already* a partaker of grace, it is that very fact 'that puts you under so binding an obligation to live 'holily?' Is such teaching as this, I ask, more likely to be perverted to the destruction of the soul than that teaching which virtually says to the sinner —'When the 'grace of Christ is given to you it will be given as an 'irresistible influence; if you have not felt that influence, 'you never have been partaker of His grace. You have 'only been baptized with water, seek a baptism of the 'Spirit, and all will be right. When you receive this 'latter Baptism you will be justified, all your sins for-'given, and you will then, and not till then, begin to live 'to God; for the new affection then implanted in you 'will infallibly subdue your whole inner man?' What is to prevent those who hear this, from going a step beyond what the teacher intends in the very direction he is leading them, and saying, 'We will wait God's time 'for our conversion, and now live as we like?' Is it not tempting them to say what Israel said of old, "What "portion have we in David? Neither have we inheri-"tance in the son of Jesse?" 'What part or lot have 'we in Christ? What interest have we in his kingdom? 'Let us live to this world till God takes our salvation 'into His own hands, and by working in us the change 'of which you speak, give us a hope that we may have a 'title to a mansion in a better?'

I cannot see how Antinomianism in the professing Church can be opposed, except by the weapon with which the apostle opposed it, that is, holding men responsible for grace already bestowed, at some definite past time;

and *that time* the word of God indicates to be the time of their Baptism.

D. But surely, by all this you necessarily depreciate the importance of any after change in the sinner who, whatever may have been the grace once bestowed on him, is now living without God.

C. No. The Church tells the Baptized sinner, living without God, that unless he repent, his condemnation will be infinitely worse, as the condemnation of one "*who* "*has received the grace of God in vain.*" She would, it is true, have men so live up, from their earliest years, to grace given, as not to need the decided change implied in Conversion. She knows that it is within the power of God to effect this, and she knows that, in one sense, it must be contrary to His will if it be otherwise, for He both hates iniquity, and His will is that *no* little one should perish, that is, should fall into the ways of sin and death. She knows that in a byegone dispensation of far less grace and privilege, God has brought this to pass in the case of such children as Samuel, and John the Baptist; and she believes that if men had faith to look for, and tenderly cherish, Baptismal grace in young children, such instances would be far more frequent. But when men *have fallen* from grace given, and *have left* their Father's house, and are *feeding* on the husks among swine, none can exhort them more urgently, or more lovingly, to *return* to their home. But she dares not make her teaching imply that it is needful that each member of Christ's Church should forsake God, and become alienated from Him, so that at some future period he may be more deeply convinced of sin, and close in more heartily with the offers of mercy. She knows who has said "Shall we continue in sin that grace may "abound? God forbid;" and by her system she makes the application of this 'God forbid,' as wide as possible.

She believes that children from their very birth are fit subjects for God's kingdom. She admits them into that kingdom in hearty faith, that when they are so admitted, God gives them, one by one, grace to live up to their new state of privilege and responsibility; she instructs them as members of Christ, and children of God. Parents, teachers, and ministers are alike enjoined to teach their precious charge that they have already received grace, and that this grace must be stirred up by exercise, preserved by watchfulness, and increased by prayer. In order to this she plies them from infancy with the same Baptismal motives to holiness, as she finds the Apostles do those under *their* charge. Her commission is not only to extend her borders, but to bring up to the second coming of our Lord, successive generations of saints united in their infancy to Christ Her Head; and as they grow up showing forth as far as possible a resemblance to Him, who "increased in wisdom and "stature, and in favour with God and man."

D. But how miserably different is the actual state of things from this exalted idea!

C. Whose fault is that? The Church in her system has from the first been most explicit with respect to the importance of Baptismal teaching, as grounded on Baptismal grace and responsibility. If both wicked and good parents have neglected her direction, — the one through carelessness, or dislike of Religion; the other, through the influence of mistaken principles, is she to blame? Yes, she would say, let the fault be mine; blame my coldness, my sinful divisions, and the scandals that cause them, all which hinder the working of God's grace; blame my want of discipline; but say not that children fall away into sin, after being brought into God's kingdom, because they have not had grace given them to live as children of the kingdom.

D. But by this doctrine do not you tie the grace of God to an action, an outward rite, performed by man; and so make the salvation of one human being dependent on the act of another?

C. No, we do not; because we believe that Baptism is not man's ordinance, but God's; that the will of him who administers it (provided he does so according to Christ's ordinance), in no way adds to, or detracts from, its efficacy; he being a mere instrument in the hands of an Unseen, but Omnipresent Saviour, who Himself favourably receives the Infants, one by one, and embraces them in the arms of His mercy. This way of viewing Baptism gives us a sufficient answer to absurd objections to all Infants receiving grace in the Sacrament, because of the unworthiness of the minister, or parents, or sponsors. They, who hold that the child's regeneration is dependent on any other circumstances than the institution of the Saviour,—baptizing with water in the name of the Father, Son, and Holy Ghost,—by holding this make the blessing dependent on man, on his intention, his faith, his feelings, his sincerity: not on the never failing promise of Christ, to be with His Church to the end of the world. One impugner of the doctrine of Baptismal Regeneration supposes a case of a worldly clergyman baptizing the child of fashionable parents in a drawing room; the remainder of the evening being spent in dancing and other frivolities, in which the clergyman and sponsors take part. He triumphantly asks, 'would God regenerate the child under such cir-'cumstances?' Another proposes a case of this sort. —An illegitimate child is brought by its mother and the parish beadle to be baptized for registration purposes; the country vicar, just come home from following the hounds, puts on his surplice, and baptizes it. 'Can 'we suppose,' he asks, 'that the child, baptized under 'such circumstances, is necessarily regenerate?'

We have seen how practically the Apostle Paul treats "the doctrine of Baptism;" how he uses the Baptism of all to whom he writes, as the strongest motive to them to live holy lives. Now supposing that in any parish there is ascertained to be a number of persons baptized under the unfavourable circumstances mentioned above; and a minister comes among them, who thinks the Apostle's method of teaching holiness the true one, and wishes to apply it to the persons so baptized. Can he do so? Is he to baptize them himself over again, before he can read to them, or apply to them individually, the doctrine contained in *Romans* vi. "Know ye not "that so many of us as were baptized into Jesus Christ "were baptized into His death;" or that doctrine which we have so repeatedly mentioned as pervading the first Epistle to the Corinthians, that they (the Corinthians) should walk warily, and live holily, because they *had* been saved, brought into Christ's body, and made partakers of His Spirit? If he does not rebaptize them, he must teach them on the faith that their former Baptism was, in all respects, as far as the responsibility to live to God was concerned, as valid as any that could be bestowed on them; and how he could do so without supposing that God conferred grace in it, I cannot imagine.

Surely persons who make such objections can never have thought of the meaning of such a passage as 2 *Corinth.* iv. 7. "We have this treasure in earthen vessels, that the excellency of the power may be of "God, and not of us."

D. This view of yours, that Baptism is not the ordinance of man, but of God, seems to meet every difficulty.

C. But do not suppose it is my view. It has been held by every divine of eminence in the Church, and by none more strongly than by one whom *you* consider to have been especially raised up by God to work a great work in His Church, *Martin Luther.* These are his words—" Baptism cannot fail to effect that for which "it was appointed, namely, regeneration and spiritual "renewal, as St Paul teaches in the third Chapter to "Titus. For as we were born into this life from Adam "and Eve, so our true man, which was before born "in sins to death, must be regenerated to righteousness "and eternal life, by the power of the Holy Ghost. "To this Regeneration and Renewal, there lacks the "application of no other external means than Water, and "Words; of the one whereof our eyes take note, our ears "of the other. Yet they have such virtue and energy, "that the man who was conceived and born in sin, "is regenerated in the view of God; and that he who "was before condemned to death, is now made truly God's "Son. This glory and virtue of Holy Baptism, who "can attain and perceive by sense, thought, and human "intellect? You should not regard, therefore, the hand "or mouth of the minister who baptizes—who pours over "the body a little water, which he has taken in the "hollow of his hand, and pronounces some few words "(a thing, slight and easy in itself, addressing itself "only to the eyes and ears; and our blinded reason "sees no more to be accomplished by the minister); "but in all this you must behold and consider the word "and work of God, by whose authority and command "Baptism is ministered, who is its founder, and author, "yea, who is himself the Baptist. And hence has "Baptism such virtue and energy (as the Holy Ghost "witnessed by St Paul) that it is the laver of Regenera- "tion, and of the renewal of the Holy Ghost; by which "laver the impure and sentenced nature which we draw "from Adam is altered and amended."

D. I will now state my last objection. Do you not think that the view you take of Baptismal Regeneration opposes the doctrine of Justification by Faith, so expressly asserted by Scripture, and by the articles of the Church of England?

C. I certainly do not. In *Romans* v. 1. St Paul asserts that "being justified by Faith, we have peace with " God through our Lord Jesus Christ." In *Romans* vi. he tells us that "we are buried with Him (Christ) " by Baptism into death : that like as Christ was raised " from the dead by the Glory of the Father, even so " we also should walk in newness of life." In *Galatians* iii. 26. he tells his converts that they " are all the children " of God by Faith in Christ Jesus, and in the next verse he assigns *as a reason* for so saying "*For* as " many of you as have been baptized into Christ, have " put on Christ." In *Hebrews* vi. he mentions consecutively as first principles, " Faith towards God," and " the doctrine of Baptisms." It is evident then that so far from considering the views he lays down of Faith and Baptism to be inconsistent, he considers both doctrines to be inseparably united. He looks upon both as essential in their places. If *you* do not think this, it is no reason that the doctrines cannot be reconciled ; but it is very strong reason for *you* to see to it that *you* are not mistaken in your estimate of one or both of them. I before read to you some remarks of Martin Luther on Baptism ; listen now, I pray you, to what he says in his Commentary on the verse of the Galatians I before alluded to (*Gal.* iii. 26, 27.) No one can question *his* attachment to the doctrine of Justification by Faith ; but he evidently saw no difficulty in holding along with it, the highest possible view of Baptismal Grace. After explaining at some length the difference between putting on Christ legally and evangelically, and shewing that in Baptism we put Him on evangelically, that is, clothe ourselves with His righteousness, he thus concludes, " Hence in Baptism the " vesture of the righteousness of the law of our own " works, is not given ; but Christ becomes our garment. " Now He is not the law, nor a lawgiver, nor work, but a " Divine and ineffable Gift which the Father has given us, " to be our Justifier, Life-giver, and Redeemer. Then " to put on Christ evangelically is not to put on the

"law and works, but an invaluable Gift, even the re-
"mission of sins, righteousness, peace, consolation, joy in
"the Holy Ghost, salvation, life, and Christ himself."

"This place is to be carefully observed, as it stands
"opposed to the fanatics, who extenuate the majesty
"of Baptism, and speak of it wickedly and impiously.
"Paul, on the contrary adorns Baptism with magnificent
"titles, calling it the washing of Regeneration and
"renewing of the Holy Ghost (Titus iii.), and here he
"says that all the Baptized have put on Christ; as
"though he said—'You have not received by Baptism
"a mark by which you are enrolled in the number
"of Christians, as many fanatics in our time think,
"who have made of Baptism only a mark, that is,
"some little empty sign;" "but as many of you,"
"he says, "as have been baptized, have put on Christ,"
"that is, you are taken beyond the law to a new nativity,
"which was done in Baptism. You are therefore no
"longer under the law, but are clothed with a new
"garment, even the righteousness of Christ." Then Paul
"teaches that Baptism is not a sign, but the garment
"of Christ; yea, that Christ himself is our garment.
"Hence Baptism is a thing very potent and efficacious.
"But when we put on Christ, the garment of our right-
"eousness and salvation, we then also put on Christ as
"the vesture of imitation." Luther on *Galatians* iii.
26, 27.

Let us now briefly advert to the leading points of
what we have been considering.

In the first place we deduced from certain passages of
Scripture the Apostolic doctrine of Baptism, that it is
the means whereby the blood of Jesus Christ is applied
for the remission of sin to those who come to it in
repentance and faith—that in the same Sacrament they
are made partakers of the benefits of Christ's death
by being buried with Him—that by it they are clothed
with Christ, and so grafted into His mystical body,
and made partakers of His Spirit, that their members are
the members of Christ, and their bodies temples of
the Spirit—that by it they are brought into a state
of salvation — in a word, that they are regenerated or
born of water and of the Spirit.

We then considered the reasons why we administer
this Sacrament to Infants, we showed that every ar-

gument we have for giving them Baptism, is equally an argument for believing, that each one of them is, at its Baptism, made a member of Christ, the child of God, and an inheritor of the kingdom of heaven, brought into a state of salvation, and made a partaker of God's Spirit. We went into this at some length with reference to the analogy of Circumcision, the encouragement given us for the Baptism of Infants by our Lord's graciously allowing them to be brought to Him, and the Baptism of households by the Apostles. We then fully, and I hope, fairly, met every objection brought against the doctrine of Regeneration of all Infants in this Sacrament, taken either from Scripture, or from considerations drawn from the present state of professing Christians. We found that some of these objections arose from the misconception or misapplication of certain passages of God's Word, and that the same unerring word supplied a ready answer to others. On these grounds then, amongst others, we affirm that the Church is fully borne out by Scripture in asserting, that every Infant is regenerated in Baptism, and by asserting this, she enables her ministers to hold their people, as the Apostles did theirs, RESPONSIBLE FOR GRACE ALREADY GIVEN, and so bound, *all of them*, by the strongest obligations, to walk in newness of life.

APPENDIX A.

No spiritual state of the Christian Church can well be imagined more miserable than that of the Jewish Church and nation in the times immediately preceding, and during the Captivity.

God, to arouse the Israelites to a sense of their need of repentance, sent to them the prophets Jeremiah & Ezekiel.

Now two ways may be supposed to have been open to these messengers of heaven, by which to call their countrymen to repentance.

They might have told them that their long continued neglect of God had so alienated God from them, that, as far at least as the great majority were concerned, God had nothing to do with them, nor they with God—They had no covenant interest in the God of Abraham—They were not *His people, His chosen*—In their present state of impenitency the endearing names of "*Jacob*" and "*Israel*" could not be applied to them.

But the door of repentance was yet mercifully open to them, and, if they turned to God with true hearts, and put away their idols, then they would, for the first time, *begin* to be counted in the number of His people,—be partakers of the privileges, and so come under the obligations, of the new covenant.

This is *one* way by which we may suppose that Jeremiah and Ezekiel would call their countrymen to come to God.

It could scarcely be called *returning* to God, for they had never, (according to this hypothesis) been in His family, or among the number of His *people*.

The other mode of speaking we might suppose these prophets to have used would be exactly the contrary. It would be to establish a claim upon them on God's part for the interest He had taken in each and all, and the interest he had given to each one in Himself by having received each of them in past time into the bonds and obligations of the covenant he had made with their great forefather.

In this latter case, instead of calling in question the fact of their being the "*Israel*" of God, they (the prophets) would use the fact of their being *Israel* to convince them of the greater sinfulness of their sin in departing from the God of Israel, and also as the reason why they should not merely *come*, but *return* to the God of Israel.

Now the few passages I have quoted indicate clearly enough that the latter mode of address was used in preference to the former, but the frequency and universality of this mode of speaking can be appreciated only by a careful perusal of these prophecies.

The following are some of the leading passages shewing that the latter mode of addressing the Israelites was adopted, and not the former.

Jer. II. 2. "Go and cry in the ears of Jerusalem, saying, thus saith "the Lord, I remember thee, the kindness of thy youth, "the love of thine espousals, when thou wentest after "me in the wilderness—Israel was holiness unto the "Lord, and the first fruits of His increase...Hear ye the "word O house of Jacob and all the families of the house "of Israel. What iniquity have your fathers found in "me that they are gone far from me."

Jer. II. 11.   " Hath a nation changed their Gods which are yet as
             " Gods ? But *my people* have changed their glory for
             " that which doth not profit.

         13.   " *My people* have committed two evils, they have for-
             " saken me the fountain of living water, and have hewed
             " them out cisterns, broken cisterns, which can hold no
             " water.

         19.   " Know therefore and see that it is an evil thing and
             " bitter that *thou hast forsaken the Lord thy God,* and
             " that my fear is not in thee, saith the Lord of Hosts.
             " *For of old I have broken thy yoke, and burst thy bonds.*
             " Yet I had planted thee a noble vine, wholly a right
             " seed, how then art thou turned into the degenerate
             " plant of a strange vine unto *Me.*

   III. 1.   " They say, If a man put away his wife and she go from
             " him, and become another man's shall he return unto
             " her again ? shall not that land be greatly polluted? but
             " thou hast played the harlot with many lovers, yet
             " *return again* unto me, saith the Lord.

         14.   " Turn, O backsliding children, saith the Lord, for I AM
             " MARRIED UNTO YOU.

         22.   " Return, ye backsliding children, and I will heal your
             " backslidings, Behold we come unto Thee, for Thou art
             " the Lord our God.

 VIII. 19.   " Is not the Lord in Zion ? Is not her King in her ?
             " Why have they provoked me to anger with their
             " graven images, and with strange vanities ?

   IX. 1.   " Oh that my head were waters, and mine eyes a fountain
             " of tears, that I might weep day and night for the slain
             " of the *daughter of my people!* Oh that I had in the
             " wilderness a lodging of wayfaring men, that I might
             " leave *my people* and go from them, for they be all
             " adulterers.

   XI. 15.   " What hath *my beloved* to do in mine house, seeing she
             " hath wrought lewdness with many, and the holy flesh
             " is passed from thee, when thou doest evil then thou
           • " rejoicest.

         16.   " The Lord called thy name, A green olive tree, fair, and
             " of goodly fruit, with the noise of a great tumult He
             " hath kindled fire upon it and the branches of it are
             " broken. For the Lord of Hosts that planted thee hath
             " pronounced evil against thee, for the evil of the house
             " of Israel, and of the house of Judah, which they have
             " done against themselves, to provoke me to anger, in
             " offering incense to Baal.

  XII. 7.   " *I have forsaken mine house, I have left mine heritage ;*
             " *I have given the dearly beloved of my soul* into the
             " hand of her enemies.
             " *Mine heritage* is unto me as a lion of the forest.

         10.   " Many pastors have destroyed *My* vineyard, they have
             " trodden *my* portion under foot.

 XIII. 11.   " For as the girdle cleaveth to the loins of a man, so have
             " I caused to cleave unto ME the WHOLE house of
             " Judah, saith the Lord, that they might be unto Me
             " for a people, and for a name and for a praise, and for
             " a glory, but they would not hear.

  XIV. 8.   " Oh the hope of Israel, the Saviour thereof in time of
             " trouble, why shouldest Thou be as a stranger in the
             " land, and as a wayfaring man that turneth aside to
             " tarry for a night.

Jer. XIV. 9. " Why shouldest thou be as a man astonished, as a
" mighty man that cannot save ? yet Thou, O Lord, art
" in the midst of us, and we are called by thy name;
" leave us not.

  21. " Do not abhor us, for thy name's sake; do not disgrace
" the throne of thy glory: remember, *break not thy*
" *covenant with us.*

Jer. XVIII. 13. " Thus saith the Lord, Ask ye now among the
" heathen, who hath heard such things? the virgin
" of Israel hath done a very horrible thing.

 XXIII. 1, 2. " Woe be unto the pastors that destroy and scatter
" the *sheep* of *my pasture* saith the Lord.

  2...." Ye have scattered *my flock* and driven them
" away...

Exactly the same mode of calling the Israelites to repentance,
because of covenant blessing made over to the whole body of them,
in past time, is adopted by Ezekiel.

Independently of the number of places in the prophet in which
the Israelites are called by God "my people" (xiii. 9, 10. xiv. 8.
11., &c.) the Jewish Church is, in the sixteenth and twenty-third
chapters, upbraided as an adulteress. Now what is it which constitutes the greater guilt of adultery above fornication, but that the
person who commits this crime, is not her own, i. e. has no right,
or power over her own body which belongs to her husband, because
of the marriage covenant into which she has entered with him ?

In the sixteenth and twenty-third chapters the Jewish Church
is upbraided as having departed from God *her* husband, and the
instances of God's kindness are recounted in order to set forth the
ingratitude of her departure.

 XVI. 6. " I passed by thee, and saw thee polluted in thine
" own blood. I said unto thee when thou wast in
" thy blood, Live; yea, I said unto thee when thou
" wast in thy blood, Live.

  8. " Now when I passed by thee, and looked upon
" thee, behold, thy time was the time of love; and
" I spread my skirt over thee, and covered thy
" nakedness: yea, I sware unto thee, and entered
" into a covenant with thee, saith the Lord God,
" and thou becamest *mine.*

  9. " Then washed I thee with water: yea, I throughly
" washed thy blood from thee, and I anointed thee
" with oil.

  10. " I clothed thee also with broidered work, &c.

  11. " I decked thee also with ornaments, &c.

  12. " Thus wast thou decked with gold and silver, and
" thy raiment was of fine linen and silk."

Under these figures must be shadowed forth very great blessings
conferred by God. Blessings conferred upon the Israelites as God's
Church, and what is a Church but a number of individuals united in
one body by their having been made partakers of certain blessings.
As the *then* Church of God they received these blessings, as the
Church they fell from them, and by so doing are judged to be guilty
of the crime of spiritual adultery.

  30. " How weak is *thine* heart, saith the Lord God,
" seeing thou doest all these things, the work of an
" imperious whorish woman. In that thou buildest
" *thine* eminent place in the head of every way,
" and makest thine high place in every street; and
" hast not been as an harlot, in that thou scornest
" hire. *But as a wife that committeth adultery,*
" *that taketh strangers instead of her husband.*"

Jer. XVI. 38. "And I will judge thee as women that break "Wedlock and shed blood, are judged."

Here then is a Church, a body of living souls, falling away, and judged as an adulteress, because God had made a covenant with, and conferred unspeakable blessings upon this body.

The Jewish Church was judged as a spiritual adulteress, because God had espoused, washed, clothed, enriched, beautified this Church, this body; now if the divine benefits indicated by this "espousing," "washing," "clothing," and "beautifying," only belonged to a certain small elect remnant of truly godly persons, where was the ungrateful adultery of the mass—the body.

I do not see how this crime of spiritual adultery of the Church because of the falling away of a large majority of the members of the Church could be brought home to the persons composing this large majority, except on the supposition that the persons composing this large majority were, bonâ fide, partakers of those covenant blessings, the falling from which constitutes the crime of spiritual adultery.

Circumcision brought each individual Jew, from his earliest youth, into these covenant relations, and so the whole nation, being circumcised, were *debtors to keep God's law.* (Gal. v. 3.)

The doctrine of the regeneration of all infants in Holy Baptism is the only way of bringing all this to bear upon the vast mass in the present Church of Jesus Christ, for "regeneration" is "grafting into a body" which God has espoused, washed, clothed, sanctified, enriched, in a far higher sense than He did His ancient Church.

B.

THE following is the testimony that a careful examination of one Epistle, the first to the Corinthians, yields to this important truth, that all the baptized are responsible for the due use of a gift of God's Spirit, by which they have been grafted into the body of Christ.

The whole tenor of the Epistle would lead us to conclude that there was no Church, respecting the moral and spiritual state of which, St Paul stood in so much fear. Both false doctrine and vicious practice were apparently unchecked by the Church, and yet there is no one of his Epistles in which the Apostle speaks more absolutely and unreservedly of the Baptismal privilege of grafting into Christ's body being common to all the Baptized.

He begins with addressing them as "the Church of God which "is at Corinth," the "sanctified in Jesus Christ," the "called to be "Saints." In chap. iii. 16. he says:—"Know *ye not* that ye are the "temple of God, and that the Spirit of God dwelleth in you."—In chap. vi. 11. "Ye are washed, ye are sanctified, ye are justified, in "the name of the Lord Jesus, and by the Spirit of our God."

In verse 15 of the same chapter: "Know ye not that your bodies "are the members of Christ." In verse 19 —"What! know ye not "that your body is the temple of the Holy Ghost, *which is in you.*"

In chap. xii. 12. 27. "By one Spirit are we *all* baptized into one "body, whether we be Jews or Gentiles, whether we be bond or free, "and have all been made to drink into one Spirit."

"Now ye are the body of Christ and members in particular."

Now let us contrast this with his language to the same persons in other passages. Chap. iii. "Ye are yet carnal: for whereas there "is among you envying, and strife, and divisions, are ye not carnal, "and walk as men."

And in the same chapter "Know ye not that ye are the temple of "God and that the Spirit of God dwelleth in you," and yet to persons

" in so exalted a state of grace he says, in the same breath, " If any
" man defile the temple of God, him shall God destroy," alluding to
the persons who were causing divisions among them, as a glance at
verses 4, 5, 6, 7. will shew; and yet he proceeds, " For the temple of
" God is holy, which temple ye are."

Again chap. v. " It is commonly repeated that there is fornication
" among you, and such fornication as is not so much as named among
" the Gentiles, that a man should have his father's wife, *and ye are*
" *puffed up.*"

Again, chap. vi. 8, 9.—"Nay, ye do wrong and defraud, and that
" your brethren. Know ye not that the unrighteous shall not inherit
" the kingdom of God ?."

The whole of the latter part of chap. vi. is full of expressions
implying that the Corinthians were (all of them) members of Christ,
and yet some might fall into very gross sin. " Now the body (v. 15.)
" is not for fornication, but for the Lord." " Know ye not that your
" bodies are the members of Christ, shall I then take the members of
" Christ and make them the members of an harlot ? God forbid."

16. " What, know ye not that he which is joined to an harlot, is
" one body, for two, saith he, shall be one flesh ? But he that is
" joined unto the Lord is one Spirit. Flee fornication." " What,
" know ye not that your body is the temple of the Holy Ghost which
" is in you, which ye have of God, and ye are not your own, &c."

From chap. viii. and x. we gather that some of these Corinthians
were not free from idolatry, or at least from scandalous compliance
with the customs of an idolatrous world.

From chap. xi. we gather that they grossly abused the Lord's
table, and so eat and drank their own condemnation, and many were
accordingly punished.

From chap. xv. we gather that some were so heretical as to deny
the resurrection of the body, and so hardened as to say " let us eat
" and drink for to-morrow we die," and some knew not God, for the
Apostle says " awake to righteousness and sin not, for some have not
" the knowledge of God.

Now supposing that St Paul held upon regeneration what many
modern divines do, could he possibly have addressed such persons in
the way that we have seen he has done ? would he not rather have
been careful *not* to have used such language to them ? would he not
rather have addressed them thus. " By your divisions, and the unre-
" proved fornication of some among you, and the idolatrous practices
" of others, and by your profanation of the Lord's supper, and by
" your want of charity, and your vain-glorious display of spiritual gifts,
" and by your denial of such a fundamental truth as the resurrection,
" and your saying, "Let us eat and drink for to-morrow we die," by all
" these things you plainly prove that the bodies of many among you
" are not the temple of the Spirit, the members of many are not the
" members of Christ, that the Baptism of many among you has been
" no more than a mere form is evidenced by your present conduct.
" God has in it conferred no grace upon you, or you would be neces-
" sarily living very differently."

" By one Spirit ye have *not* all been baptized into one body. Ye
" may have been baptized with water, but that has evidently never
" brought you into the body of Christ, the true vine, in whom are no
" fruitless branches. Seek a Baptism of the Spirit, which, if you
" have, you must necessarily live to God."

If the Apostle had held what many divines do respecting the
grace of Baptism, would not such have been his language ?

But what a contrast do his actual words (or rather those of the
Holy Spirit) present ? We find no expressions of even doubt or hesi-
tation respecting grace having been conferred on the Corinthians.

" *Know ye not* that your bodies are the temple of God, the Spirit of
" God dwelleth in you."—" Know ye not that your members are the
" members of Christ."—" For as the body is one and hath many
" members and all the members of that one body being many are one
" body so also is Christ."—" For by one Spirit *are we all baptized*
" into one body."—" Now *ye* are the body of Christ and *members*
" *in particular.*"

If it be said that the Apostle addressed the Corinthians, as
members of Christ, on the *charitable* assumption that they were
what they professed to be; I answer, that it would be in the highest
degree inconsistent with true charity to address any persons as
having such a privilege when they had it not.